THE 10 HABITS OF HIGHLY EFFECTIVE PEOPLE

Dr. Maxwell Shimba

Printed by Shimba Publishing LLC
Printed in the United States of America

TABLE OF CONTENTS

INTRODUCTION

Overview of Effectiveness and Its Importance

In a world characterized by rapid change and constant demands on our time and energy, the concept of effectiveness has never been more relevant. Effectiveness is not just about getting things done; it's about getting the right things done in the right way. It's the difference between being busy and being productive, between managing tasks and leading a fulfilling life. At its core, effectiveness is about aligning your actions with your deepest values, purpose, and long-term goals.

As individuals, our effectiveness determines our ability to influence the world around us, achieve our goals, and maintain a sense of balance and well-being. In the workplace, effectiveness is the cornerstone of productivity, innovation, and leadership. On a societal level, the effectiveness of individuals and organizations contributes to the overall progress and well-being of communities and nations.

But what does it take to be truly effective? Is it about working harder, longer, or faster? Or is it about working smarter, focusing on what truly matters, and making conscious choices that lead to meaningful outcomes? These are the questions that this book seeks to answer by exploring the habits and principles that underpin lasting effectiveness.

Brief on Stephen R. Covey's Original Work and Its Impact

In 1989, Stephen R. Covey published a book that would go on to become one of the most influential works in the field of personal development and leadership: The 7 Habits of Highly Effective People. Covey's work introduced a paradigm shift in how we think about success and effectiveness. Rather than focusing solely on external achievements or quick fixes, Covey emphasized the importance of character, principles, and long-term personal growth.

Covey's 7 Habits framework is built on the idea that effectiveness is rooted in natural laws and universal principles—such as integrity, honesty, and fairness—that govern human behavior. These habits are not just techniques for time management or productivity; they are timeless principles that, when internalized and practiced, lead to profound personal and professional transformation.

The impact of Covey's work has been immense. The 7 Habits of Highly Effective People has sold over 40 million copies worldwide and has been translated into dozens of languages. It has become a foundational text for leaders, educators, and individuals seeking to improve their lives and make a positive impact on the world. Covey's principles have been adopted in organizations of all kinds, from Fortune 500 companies to non-profits, and have inspired millions of people to live more effective, purposeful lives.

Objective of the Book

While Stephen Covey's original seven habits provide a powerful framework for personal and professional effectiveness, the world has evolved significantly since the book's first publication. New challenges, opportunities, and insights have emerged, requiring us to revisit and expand upon Covey's principles to stay relevant in today's complex and fast-paced world.

The objective of this book, The 10 Habits of Highly Effective People, is to build on the foundation laid by Covey and introduce new habits and perspectives that are crucial for effectiveness in the 21st century. We will explore the original seven habits in depth, providing fresh insights and practical applications for today's challenges. In addition, we will introduce three new habits that reflect the realities of the modern world—habits that will help you navigate change, foster innovation, and leave a lasting legacy.

This book is designed for anyone who wants to achieve more in life—not just in terms of success, but in terms of significance. Whether you are a leader seeking to inspire your team, an entrepreneur striving to make your vision a reality, or an individual looking to live a more meaningful and balanced life, the principles and habits discussed in this book will provide you with the tools you need to become more effective in all areas of your life.

As you read through these pages, I encourage you to reflect on your own habits, mindsets, and behaviors. Consider how you can apply these principles in your daily life and work, and how you can continue to grow and evolve as a person. Effectiveness is not a destination; it's a journey—a continuous process of learning, growth, and self-improvement. My hope is that this book will serve as a guide on that journey, helping you to unlock your full potential and make a meaningful impact on the world around you.

Let's begin this journey together, exploring the timeless principles of effectiveness and discovering new ways to apply them in our lives today.

This introduction sets the stage for the rest of the book by establishing the importance of effectiveness, honoring the legacy of Covey's original work, and outlining the purpose of expanding on his principles to meet the needs of the modern world.

DR. MAXWELL SHIMBA

CHAPTER 01

BE PROACTIVE

Understanding Proactivity

Proactivity is one of the most foundational principles of personal effectiveness. It is the cornerstone of all other habits because it involves taking responsibility for your life and actions rather than blaming external factors or circumstances. To understand proactivity is to understand the power you have to shape your destiny through your decisions and actions.

Definition and Importance

Proactivity, at its essence, is the ability to take initiative and act in anticipation of future problems, needs, or changes. It means being driven by values rather than moods or circumstances, choosing your response to every situation based on a clear set of guiding principles.

A proactive person does not wait for things to happen; they make things happen. They understand that, while they cannot control all events or circumstances in their lives, they can control how they respond to those events. This mindset is crucial because it shifts the focus from being a victim of circumstances to being the architect of one's life.

The importance of proactivity cannot be overstated. It's the difference between being an active participant in your life versus being a passive observer. When you are proactive, you are in control of your actions and decisions, which allows you to direct your life according to your values and goals. This level of control leads to empowerment, greater satisfaction, and a stronger sense of purpose.

In contrast, a lack of proactivity often results in a reactive lifestyle, where individuals respond to external pressures and problems rather than initiating positive change. Reactive people tend to blame others, complain about circumstances, and see themselves as victims of fate. This mentality not only stifles growth and progress but also creates a sense of helplessness and dissatisfaction.

The Difference Between Proactive and Reactive Behavior

To further understand proactivity, it is helpful to compare it with reactive behavior. While the distinction might seem subtle at first, it has profound implications for how we live our lives.

1. Proactive Behavior:

- Driven by Values and Principles: Proactive individuals operate based on their core values and principles. They have a clear sense of what is important to them, and they make decisions that align with these values. For example, if integrity is a core value, a proactive person will choose honesty in all situations, regardless of external pressures or temptations.

- Focus on Influence: Proactive people focus their time and energy on things they can control—their circle of influence. This includes their own actions, attitudes, and responses. By focusing on what they can influence, they expand their effectiveness and gradually widen their circle of influence.

- Initiative: Proactive individuals don't wait for opportunities or solutions to come to them; they take initiative to create opportunities and solve problems. They are not content with simply reacting to situations; they actively seek out ways to improve and innovate.

- Ownership and Responsibility: A proactive person takes full responsibility for their life and actions. They do not blame others or external circumstances for their problems. Instead, they recognize that their response to any situation is within their control, and they choose to act in ways that reflect their values.

- Positive Attitude: Proactive individuals maintain a positive attitude, even in challenging situations. They see obstacles as opportunities for growth and learning, and they approach problems with a solutions-oriented mindset.

2. Reactive Behavior:

- Driven by External Factors: Reactive individuals allow external factors—such as circumstances, emotions, or the behavior of others—to dictate their actions. They often act out of fear, anger, or other emotions, rather than from a place of deliberate choice.

- Focus on Concerns: Reactive people spend much of their time and energy worrying about things they cannot control—their circle of concern. This often leads to stress, frustration, and a sense of helplessness, as they focus on problems rather than solutions.

- Passivity: Reactive individuals tend to wait for things to happen before they act. They often react to situations rather than taking initiative. This passivity can lead to missed opportunities and a lack of progress in both personal and professional life.

- Blame and Excuses: A reactive person is quick to blame others or external circumstances for their problems. They often make excuses for their behavior or lack of action, which prevents them from taking responsibility and making meaningful changes.

- Negative Attitude: Reactive individuals often have a negative outlook on life. They see problems as threats rather than challenges, and they are more likely to complain about difficulties rather than finding ways to overcome them.

Real-World Examples of Proactivity

To better illustrate the concept of proactivity, consider the following real-world examples:

1. Career Development:

Imagine two employees at the same company. The first employee waits for their manager to notice their hard work and offer them a promotion. The second employee, on the other hand, proactively seeks out opportunities for growth. They take on additional responsibilities, seek feedback to improve their performance, and regularly communicate their career goals to their manager. As a result, the second employee is more likely to be promoted and advance in their career, not because they were more talented, but because they took proactive steps to make it happen.

2. Personal Health:

Consider the difference between someone who is reactive in managing their health versus someone who is proactive. A reactive person might only go to the doctor when they are already sick and might neglect healthy habits like exercise and a balanced diet until they face health issues. In contrast, a proactive individual invests in their health by exercising regularly, eating nutritious foods, and getting regular check-ups. They focus on preventing health problems before they arise, leading to better overall well-being and a higher quality of life.

3. Relationships:

In relationships, a proactive person takes the initiative to nurture and maintain strong connections with others. They don't wait for conflicts to escalate before addressing them; instead, they communicate openly and work to resolve issues early. They also make an effort to show appreciation and support for their loved ones, strengthening their relationships over time. In contrast, a reactive person might avoid difficult conversations, let problems fester, and only address issues when they become crises, often leading to strained or broken relationships.

Cultivating Proactivity

Becoming proactive is not something that happens overnight; it is a habit that must be cultivated over time. Here are some strategies to help you develop a proactive mindset:

1. Focus on What You Can Control:

Identify the areas of your life where you have influence and focus your energy there. This could be your attitude, your work ethic, your relationships, or your health.

By concentrating on what you can control, you will gradually expand your circle of influence and become more effective.

2. Set Clear Goals:

Having clear, well-defined goals gives you something to work towards and helps you stay focused on what is important. When you know what you want to achieve, you are more likely to take proactive steps to get there.

3. Take Responsibility:

Recognize that you are responsible for your life and your choices. Avoid blaming others or making excuses, and instead, take ownership of your actions and their outcomes.

4. Anticipate Challenges:

Proactive people think ahead and anticipate potential challenges. By preparing for obstacles before they arise, you can respond more effectively and avoid being caught off guard.

5. Practice Self-Reflection:

Regularly reflect on your actions and decisions. Consider how you can be more proactive in different areas of your life, and make adjustments as needed.

6. Start Small:

If you are new to the concept of proactivity, start by making small, proactive changes in your daily routine. Over time, these small changes will add up, and you will develop a more proactive approach to life.

Proactivity is more than just a habit; it is a fundamental mindset that empowers you to take control of your life and shape your destiny. By understanding the difference between proactive and reactive behavior, and by actively cultivating proactivity in your life, you can become more effective, achieve your goals, and create a life that reflects your values and aspirations.

The journey to becoming more proactive begins with a single step: recognizing that you have the power to choose your response to any situation. From there, it's about consistently making choices that align with your principles and lead you closer to the life you want to live. Remember, you are not a product of your circumstances; you are a product of your decisions. Choose to be proactive, and you will unlock the potential within you to achieve greatness.

Developing a Proactive Mindset

Proactivity is more than just a behavior—it's a mindset, a way of approaching life that influences how we think, make decisions, and interact with the world. Developing a proactive mindset is crucial for those who want to take control of their lives and achieve long-term success and fulfillment. In this chapter, we will explore the techniques for shifting from a reactive mindset to a proactive one, supported by real-life examples and case studies that illustrate the transformative power of proactivity.

Techniques for Shifting from Reactive to Proactive

1. Cultivating Self-Awareness:

- Understand Your Triggers: The first step in developing a proactive mindset is becoming aware of the situations or people that trigger reactive responses in you. These might include specific stressors at work, conflicts in personal relationships, or even certain times of the day when you feel more vulnerable to reacting impulsively. By identifying these triggers, you can start to recognize when you are slipping into a reactive mode and consciously choose a different response.

- Mindfulness Practices: Engage in mindfulness practices such as meditation, journaling, or deep-breathing exercises. These practices help you stay present, observe your thoughts and emotions without judgment, and create a space between stimulus and response. With mindfulness, you become more attuned to your internal state, which allows you to make deliberate, value-driven choices rather than impulsive, emotionally charged reactions.

2. Shifting Your Language:

- Use Proactive Language: The language you use reflects and reinforces your mindset. Reactive language often includes phrases like "I can't," "I have to," or "If only." These phrases suggest that you are at the mercy of external circumstances. In contrast, proactive language involves taking ownership of your actions and decisions, with phrases like "I choose," "I will," and "I can." By consciously adopting proactive language, you reinforce the belief that you are in control of your life.

- Reframe Negative Situations: When faced with challenges or setbacks, practice reframing the situation in a more empowering way. Instead of seeing a problem as an insurmountable obstacle, view it as an opportunity to learn and grow. For example, if a project at work fails, instead of saying, "I failed," reframe it as, "This is an opportunity to identify areas for improvement and come back stronger." Reframing helps you maintain a proactive, solutions-oriented mindset.

3. Setting Clear Goals:

- Define Your Purpose: Proactive individuals are guided by a strong sense of purpose. Take the time to reflect on your long-term goals and values. What do you want to achieve in your career, relationships, and personal growth? When you have a clear sense of purpose, you are more likely to take initiative and make decisions that align with your goals.

Your purpose acts as a compass, helping you navigate challenges and stay on course.

- Break Down Goals into Actionable Steps: Once you have defined your goals, break them down into smaller, actionable steps. A large goal can be overwhelming and may lead to procrastination, a hallmark of a reactive mindset. By breaking goals into manageable tasks, you create a clear path forward and reduce the likelihood of feeling stuck or overwhelmed. Each small step you take reinforces your proactive approach to achieving your goals.

4. Prioritizing Your Time and Energy:

- Focus on Your Circle of Influence: Proactive individuals concentrate their efforts on areas where they can make a difference—their circle of influence. Rather than worrying about things beyond your control (your circle of concern), focus on actions and decisions that are within your power. This shift in focus reduces feelings of helplessness and increases your sense of agency and effectiveness.

- Time Management Techniques: Effective time management is key to maintaining a proactive mindset. Techniques like the Eisenhower Matrix, which categorizes tasks based on urgency and importance, can help you prioritize your time effectively. By focusing on important, non-urgent tasks (such as planning, relationship-building, and personal development), you proactively prevent crises and maintain a balanced, purposeful life.

5. Taking Initiative:

- Seize Opportunities: Proactive individuals don't wait for opportunities to come to them—they create opportunities. This might involve seeking out new projects at work, volunteering for leadership roles, or initiating conversations with potential mentors. Taking initiative demonstrates that you are in control of your life and are willing to take risks to achieve your goals.

- Problem-Solving Mindset: When faced with a challenge, approach it with a problem-solving mindset. Instead of dwelling on the problem itself, focus on finding solutions. Break the problem down into smaller parts, brainstorm possible solutions, and take the first step toward resolving it. This approach shifts your focus from being overwhelmed by the problem to feeling empowered by your ability to address it.

6. Building Resilience:

- Embrace Challenges: Proactive individuals see challenges as opportunities for growth rather than threats. Cultivate resilience by developing a growth mindset, which is the belief that your abilities and intelligence can be developed through effort and learning. When you encounter obstacles, remind yourself that setbacks are a natural part of the learning process and an opportunity to build resilience and strength.

- Learn from Mistakes: Instead of fearing failure, embrace it as a valuable learning experience. Reflect on what went wrong, identify lessons learned, and apply those lessons to future situations. By viewing mistakes as opportunities for growth, you build the resilience needed to face future challenges with confidence.

Real-Life Examples and Case Studies

1. Proactive Leadership in Business:

- Case Study: Howard Schultz and Starbucks

- Howard Schultz, the former CEO of Starbucks, is a prime example of a proactive leader. When Schultz first joined Starbucks in the 1980s, the company was a small coffee bean retailer with just a few stores. However, Schultz saw an opportunity to transform Starbucks into a global brand by creating a coffeehouse culture that emphasized customer experience. He took the initiative to pitch his vision to the company's founders, and despite initial resistance, he eventually led the expansion of Starbucks into the global powerhouse it is today. Schultz's proactive mindset, vision, and willingness to take risks were instrumental in shaping the company's success.

2. Personal Growth through Proactivity:

- Example: The Story of J.K. Rowling

- J.K. Rowling, the author of the Harry Potter series, faced numerous challenges before achieving success. She was a single mother living on welfare when she began writing the first Harry Potter book. Despite facing multiple rejections from publishers, Rowling persisted, driven by her proactive mindset and belief in her work. Her determination and initiative eventually paid off when her manuscript was accepted, leading to one of the most successful literary careers in history. Rowling's story exemplifies the power of proactivity in overcoming obstacles and achieving personal goals.

3. Proactive Health Management:

- Case Study: Lance Armstrong

- Lance Armstrong, the world-renowned cyclist, was diagnosed with advanced testicular cancer in 1996. Despite the grim prognosis, Armstrong adopted a proactive approach to his treatment and recovery. He researched treatment options, sought out the best medical care, and maintained a positive, determined attitude throughout his battle with cancer. His proactive mindset not only contributed to his recovery but also inspired him to establish the Lance Armstrong Foundation (now the Livestrong Foundation) to support cancer survivors. Armstrong's proactive approach to his health and his determination to help others demonstrate the profound impact of a proactive mindset on personal well-being and community contribution.

4. Proactivity in Social Change:

- Example: Malala Yousafzai

- Malala Yousafzai, a Pakistani activist for girls' education, exemplifies proactivity in the face of adversity. At a young age, Malala began advocating for the right of girls to receive an education in Pakistan, despite threats from the Taliban. Even after surviving an assassination attempt, Malala continued her activism, speaking out on global platforms and establishing the Malala Fund to support education for girls worldwide. Her proactive stance on education has made a significant impact on the lives of many young women and has earned her the Nobel Peace Prize. Malala's story illustrates how a proactive mindset can drive social change and empower others.

Developing a proactive mindset is a transformative journey that requires conscious effort and commitment. By cultivating self-awareness, shifting your language, setting clear goals, prioritizing your time and energy, taking initiative, and building resilience, you can shift from a reactive to a proactive mindset. The real-life examples and case studies in this chapter demonstrate the power of proactivity in various aspects of life, from personal growth to leadership and social change.

As you continue to develop your proactive mindset, remember that it is a lifelong process. The more you practice these techniques, the more natural and instinctive they will become. Ultimately, a proactive mindset empowers you to take control of your life, make meaningful decisions, and achieve your fullest potential. In the next chapter, we will explore how to translate this mindset into actionable habits that can drive success and fulfillment in all areas of your life.

Creating Personal and Professional Goals

Setting goals is one of the most powerful ways to achieve success in both your personal and professional life. Goals provide direction, motivation, and a clear sense of purpose. However, not all goals are created equal. To truly be effective, goals must be set and pursued proactively. In this chapter, we will explore the principles of setting and achieving goals in a proactive manner, ensuring that your aspirations align with your values and lead to meaningful outcomes.

Setting Goals Proactively

Proactively setting goals involves taking intentional steps to define what you want to achieve and creating a plan to make it happen. Unlike reactive goal setting, where goals are often set in response to external pressures or circumstances, proactive goal setting is about aligning your goals with your values, vision, and long-term objectives. Here's how to do it:

1. Start with Your Vision:

- Define Your Long-Term Vision: Before setting specific goals, it's important to have a clear vision of what you want your life to look like in the long term. Your vision is a broad picture of your ideal future, encompassing all areas of your life, including your career, relationships, health, and personal growth. Take the time to reflect on what truly matters to you and what you want to achieve in the next 5, 10, or 20 years. This vision will serve as the foundation for your goals.

- Align with Your Values: Your goals should be a reflection of your core values. If your goals are not aligned with what you truly value, you may find yourself achieving success that feels empty or unfulfilling. For example, if one of your core values is family, a career goal that requires you to work long hours and sacrifice family time may not bring you true satisfaction. Ensure that your goals are consistent with your values and contribute to your overall sense of purpose and fulfillment.

2. Set SMART Goals:

- Specific: Clearly define what you want to achieve. Vague goals like "I want to be successful" are difficult to measure and achieve. Instead, be specific: "I want to become the Director of Marketing at my company within the next three years."

- Measurable: Ensure that your goals have measurable outcomes. This allows you to track your progress and determine when you've achieved your goal. For example, "I want to increase my sales by 20% over the next six months" is measurable, whereas "I want to improve my sales" is not.

- Achievable: Set goals that are challenging but realistic. While it's important to aim high, setting goals that are impossible to achieve can lead to frustration and discouragement. Consider your current resources, skills, and circumstances when setting goals.

- Relevant: Your goals should be relevant to your long-term vision and values. Ask yourself if achieving this goal will bring you closer to your desired future and if it aligns with what's most important to you.

- Time-bound: Set a clear deadline for achieving your goals. Having a timeline creates a sense of urgency and helps you stay focused. For example, "I want to complete my master's degree within the next two years" is a time-bound goal.

3. Break Down Goals into Actionable Steps:

- Create a Goal Hierarchy: Large goals can be overwhelming, which is why it's important to break them down into smaller, actionable steps. Start by identifying the major milestones needed to achieve your goal, and then break those milestones into specific tasks. For example, if your goal is to write a book, major milestones might include completing the outline, writing each chapter, and revising the manuscript. Each milestone can then be broken down into daily or weekly tasks.

- Set Priorities: Not all tasks are equally important, so it's essential to prioritize them. Focus on high-impact tasks that will move you closer to your goal, and tackle them first. Prioritizing tasks helps you stay on track and ensures that you're making meaningful progress toward your goal.

4. Create a Plan for Accountability:

- Track Your Progress: Regularly monitor your progress toward your goals. This could involve keeping a journal, using a project management tool, or setting up regular check-ins with yourself. Tracking your progress allows you to see how far you've come and make adjustments as needed. It also provides a sense of accomplishment and motivation as you reach each milestone.

- Seek Accountability Partners: Share your goals with someone you trust, such as a mentor, friend, or colleague. Having someone to hold you accountable can increase your commitment to your goals and provide valuable feedback and encouragement. Regular check-ins with your accountability partner can help you stay on track and address any challenges that arise.

5. Stay Flexible and Adapt:

- Embrace Change: Life is unpredictable, and circumstances can change. A proactive approach to goal setting includes being flexible and willing to adapt your goals as needed. If you encounter obstacles or if your priorities shift, don't be afraid to adjust your goals. The key is to remain focused on your long-term vision while being open to new opportunities and challenges.

- Learn from Setbacks: Setbacks and failures are a natural part of the goal-setting process. Instead of being discouraged by them, use them as opportunities to learn and grow. Analyze what went wrong, identify what you can do differently, and adjust your plan accordingly. Resilience and adaptability are essential qualities for achieving your goals proactively.

Achieving Goals Proactively

Setting goals is only the first step; achieving them requires consistent action and a proactive mindset. Here are some strategies to help you achieve your goals proactively:

1. Maintain a Positive Attitude:

- Visualize Success: Regularly visualize yourself achieving your goals. This mental rehearsal helps reinforce your commitment and keeps you motivated. Imagine the satisfaction and fulfillment you'll feel when you reach your goal, and use that vision to drive your actions.

- Stay Motivated: Motivation can wane over time, especially when pursuing long-term goals. Keep your motivation high by celebrating small wins, rewarding yourself for progress, and reminding yourself of the benefits of achieving your goal. Surround yourself with positive influences, such as supportive friends or motivational content, to keep your energy and enthusiasm up.

2. Take Consistent Action:

- Develop Daily Habits: Achieving big goals often comes down to the small, consistent actions you take every day. Identify the daily habits that will support your goals and incorporate them into your routine. For example, if your goal is to improve your fitness, a daily habit might be exercising for 30 minutes each morning.

- Avoid Procrastination: Procrastination is one of the biggest barriers to achieving goals. Combat procrastination by breaking tasks into smaller steps, setting deadlines, and using time management techniques like the

Pomodoro Technique. The key is to take action, even if it's just a small step, rather than waiting for the perfect moment.

3. Adapt to Challenges:

- Overcome Obstacles: Challenges and obstacles are inevitable when pursuing goals. Instead of seeing them as roadblocks, view them as opportunities to test your problem-solving skills and resilience. When faced with a challenge, assess the situation, brainstorm possible solutions, and take action to overcome it.

- Stay Committed: Achieving goals requires persistence and dedication, especially when things get tough. Stay committed to your goals by regularly reviewing your progress, reminding yourself of your "why," and staying focused on the bigger picture. Commitment doesn't mean never changing your goals, but it does mean staying true to your vision and being willing to put in the necessary work.

4. Reflect and Adjust:

- Regular Reflection: Periodically reflect on your progress and the effectiveness of your strategies. Are you moving closer to your goals? Are your current actions aligned with your long-term vision? Reflection helps you identify what's working and what needs to be adjusted, ensuring that you stay on the right path.

- Make Adjustments: If you find that your current plan isn't producing the desired results, don't be afraid to make adjustments. This could involve revising your goals, changing your approach, or seeking additional resources or support. Flexibility and a willingness to adapt are key to achieving your goals proactively.

Real-Life Examples and Case Studies

1. Proactive Goal Setting in Career Advancement:

- Case Study: Oprah Winfrey

- Oprah Winfrey's rise from a challenging childhood to becoming one of the most influential media personalities in the world is a testament to proactive goal setting. From a young age, Oprah had a clear vision of what she wanted to achieve, and she set specific goals to get there. She broke down her goals into actionable steps, such as pursuing a career in broadcasting, creating her talk show, and eventually founding her own media company. Throughout her journey, Oprah maintained a proactive mindset, taking initiative, adapting to challenges, and staying true to her vision.

2. Proactive Goal Achievement in Personal Growth:

- Example: Tony Robbins

- Tony Robbins, a world-renowned life coach and motivational speaker, is known for his proactive approach to personal development. Robbins sets clear goals for his personal growth, such as mastering new skills, expanding his knowledge, and improving his health. He takes consistent action by incorporating daily habits like reading, exercising, and meditating into his routine. Robbins also seeks out mentors and accountability partners to support his goals and regularly reflects on his progress, making adjustments as needed to stay on track.

3. Proactive Goal Setting in Social Change:

- Case Study: Greta Thunberg

- Greta Thunberg, a Swedish environmental activist, has demonstrated the power of proactive goal setting in driving social change. At a young age, Greta set a clear goal: to raise awareness about climate change and inspire action on a global scale. She started with small steps, such as staging a one-person protest outside the Swedish Parliament, and gradually expanded her efforts to include global climate strikes and speaking engagements at major international forums. Greta's proactive approach, driven by her values and vision, has made her a leading voice in the fight against climate change.

Creating personal and professional goals proactively is essential for achieving long-term success and fulfillment. By setting goals that align with your vision and values, breaking them down into actionable steps, and taking consistent, intentional action, you can turn your aspirations into reality. The real-life examples and case studies in this chapter illustrate the transformative power of proactive goal setting in various aspects of life.

As you continue on your journey of personal and professional growth, remember that proactive goal setting is an ongoing process. Regularly review and adjust your goals to ensure they remain relevant and aligned with your evolving vision. Stay committed to your goals, take consistent action, and embrace the challenges that come your way. With a proactive mindset and a clear plan, you can achieve anything you set your mind to. In the next chapter, we will explore how to prioritize tasks and responsibilities to ensure that you are consistently focusing on what matters most.

CHAPTER 02

BEGIN WITH THE END IN MIND

Clarifying Your Vision: Importance of Having a Clear Vision for Your Life and Career

One of the most powerful habits of highly effective people is the ability to begin with the end in mind. This principle, popularized by Stephen R. Covey, emphasizes the importance of having a clear vision of what you want to achieve in life and career. Without a clear vision, you may find yourself drifting aimlessly, reacting to circumstances rather than proactively shaping your future. This chapter delves into why having a clear vision is crucial for both your personal and professional life, and how it serves as the foundation for success and fulfillment.

The Power of Vision

Vision is the mental picture of the future you want to create. It's a vivid and compelling image of what success looks like for you. Having a clear vision gives you a sense of direction and purpose, guiding your decisions and actions toward your desired outcomes. Here's why having a clear vision is so powerful:

1. Provides Direction and Focus:

- Guiding Your Path: A clear vision acts as a roadmap for your life and career. It helps you understand where you want to go and what you need to do to get there. Without a vision, it's easy to get lost in the day-to-day tasks and lose sight of the bigger picture. Vision keeps you on course, ensuring that your efforts are aligned with your long-term goals.

- Prioritizing Your Actions: When you have a clear vision, you can prioritize your actions based on what will bring you closer to your desired future. This focus prevents you from wasting time and energy on activities that do not contribute to your goals. Instead, you can channel your resources toward the things that truly matter, making your efforts more effective and purposeful.

2. Inspires Motivation and Commitment:

- Driving Passion and Enthusiasm: A compelling vision ignites passion and enthusiasm. It gives you a reason to get out of bed each morning and work toward your dreams. This intrinsic motivation is crucial for maintaining momentum, especially when faced with challenges or setbacks. When you are deeply connected to your vision, you are more likely to stay committed and persevere through difficulties.

- Building Resilience: Life is full of obstacles and uncertainties. Having a clear vision provides you with the resilience needed to navigate these challenges. It serves as a constant reminder of why you are doing what you do, helping you to stay focused and determined even when the going gets tough.

3. Shapes Your Decisions and Actions:

- Aligning Decisions with Your Vision: Every decision you make, big or small, either moves you closer to or further away from your vision. When you have a clear vision, it becomes the standard against which you measure your choices. This alignment ensures that your decisions are consistent with your long-term goals and values, leading to more coherent and purposeful actions.

- Empowering Proactive Behavior: A clear vision empowers you to take proactive steps toward your goals. Instead of reacting to external circumstances, you can initiate actions that align with your vision. This proactive approach allows you to shape your future rather than letting it be dictated by chance.

4. Facilitates Personal and Professional Growth:

- Encouraging Continuous Improvement: A clear vision often represents a future that is beyond your current capabilities. To achieve it, you must grow, learn, and evolve. This pursuit of growth drives continuous improvement in both your personal and professional life. Whether it's acquiring new skills, expanding your knowledge, or developing better habits, your vision pushes you to become the best version of yourself.

- Fostering Innovation and Creativity: When you have a compelling vision, you are more likely to think outside the box and explore innovative ways to achieve your goals. This creativity is fueled by the desire to make your vision a reality, leading to new ideas, solutions, and approaches that you might not have considered otherwise.

5. Enhances Decision-Making and Problem-Solving:

- Providing Clarity in Decision-Making: In a world full of choices, having a clear vision simplifies decision-making. It acts as a filter, helping you distinguish between opportunities that align with your goals and those that do not. This clarity reduces indecision and helps you make choices that are in line with your long-term objectives.

- Improving Problem-Solving: When faced with challenges, a clear vision helps you stay focused on the bigger picture. It encourages you to approach problems with a solutions-oriented mindset, rather than getting bogged down by obstacles. With your vision in mind, you can find creative ways to overcome challenges and continue moving forward.

6. Creates a Sense of Purpose and Fulfillment:

- Living a Purpose-Driven Life: At the heart of a clear vision is a sense of purpose. It gives meaning to your actions and decisions, making your life more fulfilling. When you know what you are working toward and why, you experience a deeper sense of satisfaction and contentment. This purpose-driven approach to life enhances your overall well-being and happiness.

- Building a Legacy: A clear vision often extends beyond personal success to include the impact you want to have on others and the world. Whether it's contributing to your community, advancing your field, or leaving a positive legacy, your vision shapes the mark you leave on the world. This sense of contribution adds an extra layer of meaning and fulfillment to your life and career.

Examples of the Importance of Vision

To further illustrate the importance of having a clear vision, consider the following examples:

1. Vision in Personal Development:

- Example: Nelson Mandela

- Nelson Mandela had a clear vision of a free and democratic South Africa, where all people would be treated equally, regardless of race. This vision guided his life's work, even during the 27 years he spent in prison. Mandela's unwavering commitment to his vision inspired millions and ultimately led to the end of apartheid in South Africa. His life exemplifies the power of a clear vision to drive personal growth, resilience, and societal change.

2. Vision in Business Success:

- Example: Steve Jobs and Apple

- Steve Jobs had a clear vision for Apple: to create innovative and beautifully designed products that would revolutionize the way people interact with technology. This vision guided every aspect of Apple's business, from product development to marketing. Jobs' vision not only led to the creation of iconic products like the iPhone and iPad but also transformed Apple into one of the most valuable companies in the world. His vision-driven approach to business demonstrates how a clear vision can lead to extraordinary success and innovation.

3. Vision in Career Advancement:

- Example: Oprah Winfrey

- Oprah Winfrey's vision was to create a platform that would inspire and empower people to live their best lives. This vision guided her career decisions, from her work as a talk show host to her ventures in media and philanthropy.

Winfrey's commitment to her vision not only brought her immense professional success but also made a significant impact on millions of people around the world. Her career is a testament to the power of having a clear vision in achieving both personal fulfillment and professional excellence.

Steps to Clarify Your Vision

Now that we've explored the importance of having a clear vision, let's look at the steps you can take to clarify your own vision for your life and career:

1. Reflect on Your Core Values:

- Start by identifying your core values—the principles and beliefs that are most important to you. These values will serve as the foundation for your vision. Consider what truly matters to you, what you stand for, and what you want to be known for.

2. Imagine Your Ideal Future:

- Take time to visualize your ideal future. What does success look like for you in the next 5, 10, or 20 years? What do you want to achieve in your career, relationships, health, and personal growth? Be as specific and detailed as possible in your visualization.

3. Write Down Your Vision:

- Once you have a clear picture of your ideal future, write it down. Describe your vision in vivid detail, including the goals you want to achieve, the person you want to become, and the impact you want to have on others. This written vision will serve as a reference point as you make decisions and take actions toward your goals.

4. Align Your Vision with Your Actions:

- Review your current actions and decisions to ensure they align with your vision. Are you taking steps that will bring you closer to your desired future? If not, consider what changes you need to make to realign your life with your vision.

5. Revisit and Refine Your Vision:

- Your vision may evolve over time as you grow and gain new experiences. Regularly revisit and refine your vision to ensure it remains relevant and aligned with your values and goals. This ongoing process of reflection and refinement will help you stay focused on your long-term objectives.

Having a clear vision for your life and career is essential for achieving success and fulfillment. A compelling vision provides direction, motivates action, shapes decisions, and fosters personal and professional growth. It empowers you to live a purpose-driven life and make a meaningful impact on the world around you.

As you clarify your vision and begin to align your actions with your desired future, you will find that your life becomes more focused, purposeful, and fulfilling. In the next section, we will explore how to create a personal mission statement that encapsulates your vision and serves as a guiding star for your life's journey.

Techniques for Defining Your Personal and Professional End Goals

Setting personal and professional end goals is a crucial step in achieving success and fulfillment in life. These goals act as the destination you are working toward, providing clarity and direction in your journey. However, defining these end goals requires careful thought, reflection, and planning. In this chapter, we will explore various techniques for effectively defining your personal and professional end goals, ensuring they are aligned with your values, vision, and long-term aspirations.

Understanding End Goals

End goals are the ultimate outcomes you want to achieve in your life and career. They represent the culmination of your efforts, guiding your decisions and actions along the way. Unlike short-term or intermediate goals, which may change as circumstances evolve, end goals are more stable and reflect your deepest desires and aspirations.

1. Clarifying Your Core Values:

- Identify What Matters Most: The foundation of defining your end goals lies in understanding your core values. These are the principles and beliefs that guide your life, influencing your decisions, behaviors, and overall sense of purpose. Begin by reflecting on what matters most to you. Ask yourself questions like:

- What do I stand for?

- What brings me the most fulfillment and satisfaction?

- What kind of person do I want to be remembered as?

- Align Goals with Values: Once you have identified your core values, ensure that your end goals are aligned with them. For example, if one of your core values is helping others, your end goal might involve making a significant impact through philanthropy or community service. When your goals are rooted in your values, you are more likely to find meaning and motivation in pursuing them.

2. Visualizing Your Ideal Future:

- Create a Vision Board: One effective technique for defining your end goals is to create a vision board. A vision board is a visual representation of your ideal future, including images, words, and symbols that resonate with your goals and aspirations. This tool helps you clarify what you want to achieve by making your goals tangible and real. To create a vision board:

- Gather magazines, images, and other materials that inspire you.

- Cut out pictures and words that represent your dreams and goals.

- Arrange them on a board in a way that feels meaningful to you.

- Place your vision board somewhere visible to keep your goals top of mind.

- Use Visualization Exercises: In addition to a vision board, you can practice visualization exercises to help you define your end goals. Spend time each day imagining yourself having achieved your goals. Picture what your life looks like, how you feel, and the impact you've made. Visualization helps solidify your goals in your mind, making them more concrete and achievable.

3. Setting SMART Goals:

- Specific: Define your goals with precision. Instead of vague aspirations like "I want to be successful," specify what success looks like to you. For example, "I want to become the CEO of a technology company by age 40" is a specific goal that gives you a clear target to aim for.

- Measurable: Ensure that your goals can be measured. This allows you to track your progress and know when you've achieved your goal. For instance, if your goal is to improve your health, you might measure it by aiming to lose a certain amount of weight or complete a marathon.

- Achievable: Set goals that are realistic and attainable, considering your current resources, skills, and circumstances. While it's important to challenge yourself, setting unattainable goals can lead to frustration and demotivation.

- Relevant: Your goals should be relevant to your long-term vision and aligned with your core values. This relevance ensures that your efforts are focused on what truly matters to you.

- Time-bound: Assign a deadline to your goals. Having a time frame creates a sense of urgency and motivates you to take action. For example, "I want to publish my first book by December 2025" is a time-bound goal that gives you a clear deadline to work toward.

4. Breaking Down Goals into Milestones:

- Identify Key Milestones: Once you've defined your end goals, break them down into smaller, manageable milestones. Milestones are intermediate steps that lead you closer to your ultimate goal. For example, if your end goal is to start your own business, key milestones might include completing a business plan, securing funding, and launching your first product.

- Create an Action Plan: Develop an action plan that outlines the specific tasks and steps needed to achieve each milestone. This plan should include deadlines, resources required, and potential obstacles you might encounter. An action plan helps you stay organized and focused, ensuring that you make steady progress toward your end goals.

5. Incorporating Flexibility:

- Adapt to Change: While it's important to set clear end goals, it's equally important to remain flexible and open to change. Life is unpredictable, and circumstances may require you to adjust your goals along the way. Embrace change as an opportunity for growth and be willing to revise your goals if needed.

- Regularly Review Your Goals: Periodically review your end goals to ensure they remain relevant and aligned with your evolving vision. As you grow and gain new experiences, your goals may shift. Regular reflection allows you to make necessary adjustments and stay on track.

6. Seeking Feedback and Mentorship:

- Consult with Trusted Advisors: Seek feedback from mentors, colleagues, or trusted advisors as you define your end goals. Their insights can provide valuable perspective, helping you refine your goals and identify potential challenges. Mentors can also offer guidance and support as you work toward your goals.

- Engage in Peer Discussions: Engage in discussions with peers who share similar aspirations. Sharing your goals with others can provide motivation and accountability, as well as opportunities for collaboration and learning.

7. Balancing Personal and Professional Goals:

- Integrate Personal and Professional Aspirations: It's important to consider both personal and professional goals when defining your end goals. A fulfilling life involves a balance between career success and personal well-being. For example, if your professional goal is to advance in your career, consider how it aligns with your personal goals for family life, health, and personal growth.

- Set Complementary Goals: Aim to set goals that complement rather than conflict with each other. For instance, if one of your personal goals is to maintain a healthy work-life balance, your professional goals should support this, perhaps by focusing on productivity and efficiency rather than long hours.

8. Harnessing the Power of Purpose:

- Define Your Purpose: Your purpose is the underlying reason for pursuing your goals. It's the "why" behind what you do. Take time to reflect on your purpose and how it connects to your end goals. For example, if your purpose is to make a positive impact on the environment, your end goals might include leading a sustainable business or advocating for environmental causes.

- Align Goals with Purpose: Ensure that your goals are aligned with your purpose. When your goals are driven by a sense of purpose, you are more likely to stay motivated and committed, even in the face of challenges. Purpose-driven goals lead to greater fulfillment and a stronger sense of achievement.

9. Documenting and Communicating Your Goals:

- Write Down Your Goals: Writing down your goals makes them tangible and real. It also serves as a constant reminder of what you are working toward. Consider keeping a goal journal where you document your goals, milestones, and progress. This journal can also serve as a tool for reflection and adjustment.

- Communicate Your Goals: Share your goals with others, whether it's with a mentor, partner, or close friend. Communicating your goals can increase accountability and provide additional support and encouragement. When others are aware of your goals, they can offer valuable advice and help you stay on track.

10. Celebrating Successes:

- Acknowledge Milestones: As you achieve each milestone on the way to your end goals, take time to celebrate your success. Acknowledging your progress reinforces positive behavior and keeps you motivated. Celebrating small wins also boosts your confidence and provides momentum for the next steps.

- Reflect on Achievements: After reaching your end goals, reflect on your journey and the lessons learned along the way. Consider how your achievements have impacted your life and how they align with your vision and purpose. This reflection helps you appreciate your hard work and prepares you for setting new goals in the future.

Real-Life Examples of Defining End Goals

To illustrate the importance and effectiveness of defining end goals, consider the following real-life examples:

1. Personal End Goals:

- Example: Mahatma Gandhi

- Mahatma Gandhi had a clear personal end goal: to achieve independence for India through non-violent resistance. This goal was deeply rooted in his core values of peace, justice, and equality. Gandhi's unwavering commitment to his goal guided his actions and decisions throughout his life, ultimately leading to India's independence in 1947. His life demonstrates the power of having a well-defined end goal and the impact it can have on both personal fulfillment and societal change.

2. Professional End Goals:

- Example: Elon Musk

- Elon Musk's professional end goal is to revolutionize transportation and colonize Mars, driven by his vision of making life multi-planetary. This ambitious goal has shaped his career and led to the founding of companies like SpaceX and Tesla. Musk's ability to define and pursue audacious end goals has positioned him as a leader in technology and innovation, illustrating the importance of having clear, purpose-driven professional goals.

3. Balancing Personal and Professional Goals:

- Example: Sheryl Sandberg

- Sheryl Sandberg, COO of Facebook, has successfully balanced her personal and professional goals. Her professional end goals include advancing women's leadership and fostering a more inclusive workplace, while her personal goals focus on family and personal well-being. Sandberg's ability to integrate and align her personal and professional goals has enabled her to achieve success in both areas, serving as a model for others seeking to balance their aspirations.

Defining your personal and professional end goals is a vital step in achieving a fulfilling and successful life. By clarifying your core values, visualizing your ideal future, setting SMART goals, and breaking them down into actionable steps, you can create a clear path toward your desired outcomes. Incorporating flexibility, seeking feedback, and balancing your goals ensures that they remain relevant and aligned with your evolving vision.

As you continue on your journey, remember that your end goals should be driven by a sense of purpose and aligned with what truly matters to you. Document and communicate your goals, celebrate your successes, and remain open to growth and change. With well-defined end goals, you are empowered to live a life of intention, purpose, and fulfillment.

In the next section, we will explore the importance of creating a personal mission statement that encapsulates your end goals and serves as a guiding star for your life's journey.

Creating a Personal Mission Statement: Steps to Craft and Refine a Mission Statement

A personal mission statement is a powerful tool that defines your purpose, guides your decisions, and shapes your actions. It serves as a compass, helping you stay aligned with your values and long-term goals, even in the face of challenges and distractions. Crafting a personal mission statement requires deep reflection and thoughtful consideration of who you are, what you stand for, and what you want to achieve in life. In this chapter, we will explore the steps to create and refine a mission statement that resonates with your core identity and serves as a guiding star for your journey.

Step 1: Reflect on Your Core Values and Beliefs

The foundation of any mission statement lies in your core values and beliefs. These are the principles that define who you are and what you stand for. Before you can articulate your mission, you need to have a clear understanding of these foundational elements.

- Identify Your Core Values: Start by making a list of your core values. These might include honesty, integrity, compassion, family, creativity, or social justice. Think about the principles that consistently guide your decisions and behavior, and consider the values that are most important to you in your personal and professional life.

- Consider Your Beliefs: Reflect on your beliefs about life, people, and the world. What do you believe is the purpose of life? What role do you believe you should play in your community, family, or profession? Your beliefs will inform the broader perspective of your mission statement and help you articulate your sense of purpose.

Example:

If one of your core values is compassion, and you believe in the importance of helping others, your mission statement might emphasize your commitment to serving others and making a positive impact on their lives.

Step 2: Define Your Purpose

Your purpose is the overarching reason for your existence—the "why" behind everything you do. Defining your purpose is essential for crafting a mission statement that is meaningful and motivating.

- Ask Purpose-Driven Questions: To uncover your purpose, ask yourself deep and introspective questions such as:

  - What brings me the most fulfillment in life?

  - What am I passionate about?

  - How do I want to make a difference in the world?

  - What legacy do I want to leave behind?

  - What would I want people to say about me at the end of my life?

  - Identify Your Passions and Talents: Your purpose is often closely tied to your passions and talents. Think about the activities that energize you and the skills that come naturally to you. Consider how these passions and talents can be used to serve others and contribute to something greater than yourself.

Example:

If your passion is teaching and you have a natural talent for communication, your purpose might involve educating and inspiring others to reach their full potential.

Step 3: Consider Your Long-Term Goals

Your mission statement should align with your long-term goals, providing a sense of direction and focus. These goals represent the future you want to create and the milestones you want to achieve along the way.

- Visualize Your Ideal Future: Imagine your life 10, 20, or 30 years from now. What do you want to have accomplished? What kind of person do you want to be? Where do you want to be in your career, relationships, and personal development? This visualization will help you identify the goals that are most important to you.

- Align Goals with Your Mission: Ensure that your mission statement reflects your long-term goals. For example, if one of your long-term goals is to become a leader in your industry, your mission statement might emphasize your commitment to continuous learning, innovation, and leadership.

Example:

If your long-term goal is to start a nonprofit organization that supports underprivileged children, your mission statement might focus on your dedication to empowering and uplifting those in need.

Step 4: Write the First Draft

With a clear understanding of your values, purpose, and goals, you are now ready to begin writing the first draft of your mission statement. This draft will serve as the foundation that you will refine over time.

- Start with a Strong Opening: Begin your mission statement with a strong, declarative statement that captures the essence of who you are and what you stand for. This opening should be both inspiring and reflective of your core identity.

- Incorporate Key Elements: As you write, incorporate the key elements you've identified—your values, purpose, and long-term goals. Be sure to express these elements in a way that is authentic and true to who you are.

- Keep It Concise and Focused: A mission statement should be concise and to the point. Aim for a length of one to three sentences that clearly convey your mission without unnecessary complexity. Focus on the most important aspects of your mission and avoid being overly vague or general.

Example:

"My mission is to lead with integrity, inspire positive change, and empower others to achieve their fullest potential through education and mentorship."

Step 5: Reflect and Revise

Writing a mission statement is an iterative process. After completing your first draft, take the time to reflect on what you've written and make any necessary revisions. This step ensures that your mission statement is both meaningful and aligned with your true self.

- Set It Aside and Reflect: After writing your first draft, set it aside for a few days. This break allows you to return to your statement with fresh eyes and a clear perspective. As you review your statement, ask yourself whether it accurately reflects your values, purpose, and goals.

- Seek Feedback: Share your draft with trusted friends, family members, or mentors who know you well. Ask for their honest feedback on whether your mission statement resonates with who you are and what you want to achieve. Consider their suggestions, but ensure that the final statement is authentically yours.

- Revise for Clarity and Impact: Based on your reflections and feedback, revise your mission statement to enhance its clarity and impact. Ensure that each word is intentional and that the statement as a whole is both inspiring and actionable. The goal is to create a mission statement that you can confidently embrace as a guiding force in your life.

Example of Revision:

First Draft: "I want to help people and be a good leader."

Revised: "My mission is to lead with compassion, inspire positive change, and empower individuals to reach their highest potential through education and service."

Step 6: Internalize and Live Your Mission Statement

Once you have crafted and refined your mission statement, the next step is to internalize it and incorporate it into your daily life. A mission statement is not just a set of words; it's a commitment to living according to your values and purpose.

- Memorize Your Mission Statement: Internalizing your mission statement begins with memorizing it. This helps embed it into your consciousness, making it a constant reminder of who you are and what you stand for. Recite it to yourself regularly, especially when making decisions or facing challenges.

- Use It as a Decision-Making Tool: Your mission statement should guide your decisions, helping you choose actions that are aligned with your values and goals. When faced with important decisions, ask yourself whether the choice is consistent with your mission. If it is, move forward with confidence. If not, reconsider your options.

- Reflect on Your Mission Regularly: Regularly reflect on your mission statement to ensure that you are living in alignment with it. This reflection can be part of a daily or weekly practice, where you review your actions and choices in light of your mission. If you find that you've strayed from your mission, use this reflection as an opportunity to realign and recommit.

Example:

If your mission is to empower others through education, consider how your daily actions—such as mentoring a colleague, volunteering at a local school, or pursuing further education—align with this mission. Regular reflection will help you stay true to your purpose and continuously grow in your commitment to your mission.

Step 7: Revise as You Grow

Your mission statement is a living document that may evolve as you grow and experience new stages in life. Periodically revisiting and revising your mission statement ensures that it remains relevant and aligned with your evolving values, goals, and circumstances.

- Embrace Change: As you go through different phases of life—such as changing careers, starting a family, or pursuing new passions—your mission statement may need to evolve. Embrace this change as a natural part of your personal growth and be open to revising your statement accordingly.

- Regularly Review Your Mission Statement: Set aside time each year to review your mission statement. During this review, consider whether your statement still resonates with you and reflects your current values and goals. If necessary, make adjustments to ensure it continues to serve as an effective guide for your life.

- Celebrate Progress: As you revise your mission statement over time, take a moment to celebrate the progress you've made and the growth you've experienced. Recognizing your achievements reinforces the importance of living according to your mission and inspires you to continue striving for your goals.

Example of Revision Over Time:

Early Career: "My mission is to build a successful career in finance and contribute to the growth of my organization."

Mid-Career: "My mission is to lead with integrity, mentor the next generation of financial professionals, and make a meaningful impact on the industry."

Crafting and refining a personal mission statement is a powerful process that helps you clarify your purpose, align your actions with your values, and stay focused on your long-term goals. By following the steps outlined in this chapter—reflecting on your core values, defining your purpose, considering your long-term goals, writing and revising your statement, internalizing and living it, and revising it as you grow—you can create a mission statement that serves as a guiding star for your life's journey.

Your mission statement is more than just words on paper; it's a commitment to living with intention, purpose, and authenticity. As you continue to refine and live by your mission, you will find that it provides clarity, motivation, and a sense of direction, helping you navigate life's challenges and opportunities with confidence and purpose.

In the next chapter, we will explore how to align your daily actions with your mission statement to ensure that you are consistently moving toward your desired future and living a life that reflects your true self.

Aligning Daily Actions with Your Mission

Creating a personal mission statement is a powerful step toward defining your purpose and setting the course for your life. However, the true value of a mission statement lies in its application—how well it guides your daily actions and decisions. Aligning your daily actions with your mission is essential for living a life that is consistent with your values, goals, and aspirations. In this chapter, we will explore practical strategies for integrating your mission statement into your daily life, ensuring that every action you take moves you closer to fulfilling your mission.

The Importance of Alignment

Before diving into specific strategies, it's important to understand why aligning your daily actions with your mission is so crucial:

1. Consistency Between Values and Actions:

- Alignment ensures that your actions reflect your core values and beliefs. When your daily choices are consistent with your mission, you build integrity and authenticity in your life. This consistency strengthens your sense of identity and purpose, leading to greater fulfillment and satisfaction.

2. Focused Progress Toward Goals:

- A clear alignment between your actions and mission keeps you focused on your long-term goals. It helps you avoid distractions and stay on course, ensuring that your efforts are directed toward what truly matters to you. This focus increases your effectiveness and accelerates your progress toward achieving your aspirations.

3. Enhanced Decision-Making:

- When your actions are aligned with your mission, decision-making becomes simpler and more intuitive. Your mission statement serves as a guidepost, helping you choose actions that are in line with your values and goals. This alignment reduces the stress and confusion often associated with making difficult choices.

4. Increased Motivation and Resilience:

- Aligning your daily actions with your mission boosts your motivation and resilience. When you know that your efforts are contributing to a larger purpose, you are more likely to stay motivated, even in the face of challenges. This sense of purpose also helps you bounce back from setbacks and persevere through difficulties.

Strategies for Aligning Daily Actions with Your Mission

1. Start Your Day with Intention:

- Morning Reflection: Begin each day with a moment of reflection on your mission statement. Take a few minutes to remind yourself of your core values, purpose, and long-term goals. This practice helps set a positive and focused tone for the day, ensuring that your actions are aligned with your mission from the start.

- Set Daily Intentions: In addition to reflecting on your mission, set specific intentions for the day that align with your mission statement. These intentions should guide your actions and decisions throughout the day. For example, if your mission involves leading with compassion, you might set an intention to listen actively and offer support to a colleague in need.

2. Prioritize Tasks Based on Your Mission:

- Use the Eisenhower Matrix: The Eisenhower Matrix is a time management tool that helps you prioritize tasks based on their urgency and importance. Tasks that align with your mission are often both important and non-urgent, meaning they contribute to your long-term goals but don't require immediate attention. Prioritize these tasks to ensure that you are consistently making progress toward your mission.

- Create a Daily To-Do List: Develop a daily to-do list that includes tasks directly related to your mission statement. As you complete each task, reflect on how it contributes to your mission. This practice reinforces the connection between your daily actions and your long-term goals, making your efforts more purposeful and rewarding.

3. Incorporate Your Mission into Decision-Making:

- Use Your Mission as a Filter: Whenever you face a decision, whether big or small, use your mission statement as a filter. Ask yourself, "Does this choice align with my mission? Will it help me fulfill my purpose and move closer to my goals?" If the answer is yes, proceed with confidence. If not, consider alternatives that are more aligned with your mission.

- Practice Mindful Decision-Making: Mindfulness involves being fully present and aware of your thoughts, feelings, and surroundings. By practicing mindful decision-making, you can ensure that your choices are intentional and aligned with your mission. Take a moment to pause and reflect before making decisions, especially those that could have a significant impact on your life or career.

4. Stay Accountable to Your Mission:

- Track Your Progress: Regularly track your progress toward your mission by reviewing your actions and accomplishments. Consider keeping a journal where you document how your daily actions align with your mission statement. This practice helps you stay accountable and provides a tangible record of your growth and progress.

- Seek Feedback from Others: Share your mission statement with trusted friends, family members, or mentors who can hold you accountable. Ask for their feedback on how well your actions align with your mission and whether they see areas for improvement. Accountability from others can provide valuable perspective and keep you on track.

5. Create Habits that Support Your Mission:

- Identify Key Habits: Habits are the building blocks of daily life. Identify key habits that directly support your mission statement and incorporate them into your routine. For example, if your mission involves lifelong learning, make a habit of reading or taking courses regularly. Consistent habits ensure that your actions are aligned with your mission on a daily basis.

- Use Habit Stacking: Habit stacking involves linking a new habit to an existing one, making it easier to incorporate into your routine. For instance, if your mission involves leading a healthy lifestyle, you might stack a new habit of exercising with an existing habit of drinking your morning coffee. This technique makes it easier to maintain habits that align with your mission.

6. Reflect and Adjust Regularly:

- Weekly Reflection: Set aside time each week to reflect on how well your actions aligned with your mission. Consider what went well, what challenges you faced, and how you can improve. This reflection helps you stay focused and make adjustments as needed to stay on track.

- Adjust as Needed: Life is dynamic, and your circumstances, priorities, and goals may change over time. Be open to adjusting your actions and habits to better align with your mission as you grow and evolve. Regular reflection ensures that your actions remain relevant and aligned with your current mission.

7. Infuse Your Work with Your Mission:

- Align Professional Goals with Your Mission: If you're in a leadership role, consider how you can align your professional goals with your personal mission statement. For example, if your mission involves promoting social justice, look for ways to incorporate this value into your work, such as advocating for diversity and inclusion in your organization.

- Find Meaning in Everyday Tasks: Even routine tasks can be infused with meaning when they are connected to your mission. For example, if your mission involves fostering meaningful connections, approach everyday interactions—like meetings, emails, or conversations—with the intention of building and strengthening relationships.

8. Balance Productivity with Purpose:

- Avoid Over-Scheduling: While it's important to be productive, it's equally important to ensure that your productivity aligns with your mission. Avoid over-scheduling yourself with tasks that may not contribute to your long-term goals. Instead, focus on quality over quantity, prioritizing actions that have the most significant impact on your mission.

- Take Time for Self-Care: Aligning your actions with your mission requires energy and focus. Ensure that you are taking time for self-care, rest, and rejuvenation. When you are well-rested and balanced, you are better equipped to take actions that are aligned with your mission and purpose.

9. Celebrate Small Wins:

- Acknowledge Progress: Recognize and celebrate the small wins that occur when your actions align with your mission. These victories, no matter how small, reinforce positive behavior and motivate you to continue striving toward your goals. Celebrating progress also helps maintain a positive mindset, making it easier to stay aligned with your mission.

- Share Your Success: Consider sharing your successes with others, whether through social media, in conversations with friends, or within your professional network. Sharing your achievements can inspire others to align their actions with their own missions and creates a sense of community and support.

Real-Life Examples of Alignment

To illustrate how aligning daily actions with a mission statement can lead to success and fulfillment, consider the following real-life examples:

1. Oprah Winfrey:

- Oprah Winfrey's mission is centered on empowering others to live their best lives through education, inspiration, and entertainment. Throughout her career,

Winfrey has consistently aligned her daily actions with this mission, whether through her talk show, book club, or philanthropic efforts. By staying true to her mission, Winfrey has built a legacy of positive impact and continues to inspire millions around the world.

2. Elon Musk:

- Elon Musk's mission involves advancing technology to benefit humanity, particularly through sustainable energy and space exploration. Every aspect of Musk's work, from Tesla to SpaceX, is aligned with this mission. Musk's ability to consistently align his daily actions with his mission has driven innovation and positioned him as a leader in multiple industries.

3. Mother Teresa:

- Mother Teresa's mission was to serve the poorest of the poor and provide care for those who were suffering. Every action she took, from founding the Missionaries of Charity to personally caring for the sick, was aligned with this mission. Her unwavering commitment to her mission earned her global recognition and left a lasting impact on countless lives.

Aligning your daily actions with your mission is essential for living a life of purpose, integrity, and fulfillment. By starting your day with intention, prioritizing tasks that align with your mission, incorporating your mission into decision-making, and creating supportive habits, you can ensure that your actions consistently reflect your values and goals.

Regular reflection and adjustment, along with a focus on balancing productivity with purpose, help you stay on track and maintain alignment with your mission. As you continue to integrate your mission into your daily life, you will find that your actions become more intentional, your decisions more confident, and your progress more meaningful.

CHAPTER 03

PUT FIRST THING FIRST

Prioritizing Tasks and Responsibilities: The Eisenhower Matrix and Its Application

In our fast-paced world, the ability to prioritize tasks and responsibilities is essential for achieving success and maintaining balance in life. With countless demands on our time and energy, it's easy to become overwhelmed, distracted, or reactive. To effectively manage our time and focus on what truly matters, we need a reliable method for prioritizing our tasks. One of the most effective tools for this purpose is the Eisenhower Matrix, a time management framework that helps us distinguish between what is urgent and what is important. In this chapter, we will explore the Eisenhower Matrix in depth, including its origins, components, and practical applications in daily life.

Understanding the Eisenhower Matrix

The Eisenhower Matrix, also known as the Urgent-Important Matrix, is named after Dwight D. Eisenhower, the 34th President of the United States and a five-star general during World War II. Eisenhower was known for his exceptional ability to prioritize tasks and make critical decisions under pressure. He famously said, "What is important is seldom urgent, and what is urgent is seldom important." This insight led to the development of the Eisenhower Matrix, a simple yet powerful tool for prioritizing tasks based on their urgency and importance.

The Eisenhower Matrix divides tasks into four quadrants, each representing a different level of urgency and importance:

1. Quadrant I: Urgent and Important

2. Quadrant II: Not Urgent but Important

3. Quadrant III: Urgent but Not Important

4. Quadrant IV: Not Urgent and Not Important

Each quadrant requires a different approach, and understanding how to allocate tasks accordingly is key to effective time management.

Quadrant I: Urgent and Important

Description:

Quadrant I tasks are both urgent and important. These are tasks that require immediate attention and have significant consequences if not addressed promptly. They often include crises, pressing problems, and deadlines.

Examples:

- Responding to a critical issue at work (e.g., a major client complaint).

- Handling a personal emergency (e.g., a medical crisis).

- Meeting a deadline for a high-priority project.

Approach:

- Do It Now: Tasks in Quadrant I should be tackled immediately. Because they are both urgent and important, they cannot be postponed without serious consequences. The key is to handle these tasks efficiently and effectively, without allowing them to consume all of your time and energy.

Application:

- Time Blocking: Allocate specific blocks of time in your schedule to address Quadrant I tasks. This ensures that you have dedicated time to manage urgent and important matters without being constantly interrupted by less critical tasks.

- Crisis Management: Develop strategies for managing crises effectively, such as having contingency plans in place and maintaining open communication with relevant stakeholders. By being prepared, you can handle Quadrant I tasks more efficiently and reduce the likelihood of future crises.

Quadrant II: Not Urgent but Important

Description:

Quadrant II tasks are important but not urgent. These tasks contribute significantly to your long-term goals and personal growth, but they do not require immediate action. Quadrant II is often referred to as the "Quadrant of Quality" because it focuses on activities that lead to long-term success and fulfillment.

Examples:

- Planning and setting long-term goals.

- Building and maintaining relationships.

- Engaging in personal development (e.g., learning new skills, exercising, reading).

- Preventative maintenance (e.g., regular health check-ups, financial planning).

Approach:

- Schedule It: Quadrant II tasks should be scheduled into your routine. Because they are not urgent, they are often neglected in favor of more pressing but less important tasks. However, focusing on Quadrant II activities is essential for preventing future crises (Quadrant I) and for achieving long-term success.

Application:

- Daily and Weekly Planning: Incorporate Quadrant II tasks into your daily and weekly planning. Set aside time for activities that contribute to your long-term goals, such as exercise, learning, and relationship-building. By making these tasks a regular part of your routine, you ensure that they receive the attention they deserve.

- Focus on Growth: Prioritize activities that foster personal and professional growth. For example, invest time in developing new skills, attending workshops, or building a network of supportive relationships. These efforts pay off in the long run by enhancing your capabilities and expanding your opportunities.

Quadrant III: Urgent but Not Important

Description:

Quadrant III tasks are urgent but not important. These tasks demand your immediate attention but do not significantly contribute to your long-term goals. They often include interruptions, distractions, and activities that are important to others but not necessarily to you.

Examples:

- Answering non-essential phone calls or emails.

- Attending meetings that do not add value.

- Responding to requests that are not aligned with your priorities.

Approach:

- Delegate or Decline: Whenever possible, delegate Quadrant III tasks to others who are better suited to handle them. If delegation is not an option, consider whether you can decline or minimize your involvement. The goal is to reduce the time spent on tasks that are urgent for others but not important for you.

Application:

- Set Boundaries: Establish clear boundaries to protect your time and energy. For example, limit the time you spend on email or social media, and be selective about the meetings you attend. Politely decline requests that do not align with your priorities, and focus on tasks that truly matter to you.

- Use Technology Wisely: Leverage technology to automate or streamline Quadrant III tasks. For instance, use email filters to prioritize important messages and reduce the clutter in your inbox. Automating routine tasks can free up more time for activities in Quadrants I and II.

Quadrant IV: Not Urgent and Not Important
Description:

Quadrant IV tasks are neither urgent nor important. These are activities that do not contribute to your goals and often serve as distractions or time-wasters. While some Quadrant IV activities may provide temporary relief from stress, spending too much time in this quadrant can lead to unproductive and unfulfilled life.

Examples:

- Excessive time spent on social media or watching TV.

- Engaging in gossip or trivial conversations.

- Participating in activities that offer no real value or satisfaction.

Approach:

- Eliminate or Minimize: Quadrant IV tasks should be minimized or eliminated altogether. These activities do not contribute to your success or well-being, and they often detract from more meaningful pursuits. By reducing the time spent in Quadrant IV, you can redirect your energy toward tasks that are aligned with your mission and goals.

Application:

- Identify Time-Wasters: Conduct a time audit to identify activities that fall into Quadrant IV. Once you've identified these time-wasters, take steps to minimize or eliminate them from your daily routine. For example, set limits on screen time or remove distractions from your workspace.

- Replace with Meaningful Activities: Replace Quadrant IV activities with more meaningful and fulfilling pursuits. For example, instead of spending hours on social media, use that time to read, exercise, or engage in a hobby that brings you joy and satisfaction.

Practical Application of the Eisenhower Matrix

Now that we've explored each quadrant of the Eisenhower Matrix, let's look at how you can apply this tool in your daily life:

1. Create Your Matrix:

- Draw the Matrix: Start by drawing a simple four-quadrant grid on a piece of paper or using a digital tool. Label each quadrant according to the Eisenhower Matrix: Quadrant I (Urgent and Important), Quadrant II (Not Urgent but Important), Quadrant III (Urgent but Not Important), and Quadrant IV (Not Urgent and Not Important).

- List Your Tasks: Write down all of your current tasks and responsibilities in the appropriate quadrant. Be honest with yourself about where each task belongs. This exercise helps you gain clarity on how you are currently spending your time and energy.

2. Prioritize and Schedule:

- Focus on Quadrants I and II: Once you've categorized your tasks, prioritize those in Quadrants I and II. These are the tasks that will have the most significant impact on your success and well-being. Schedule time in your calendar to address these tasks first.

- Delegate or Decline Quadrant III Tasks: Look for opportunities to delegate or decline tasks in Quadrant III. If a task is urgent but not important, consider whether someone else can handle it or if you can minimize your involvement. Freeing up time in this quadrant allows you to focus on more important activities.

- Eliminate Quadrant IV Tasks: Identify tasks in Quadrant IV and take steps to eliminate or reduce them. Redirect the time you would have spent on these tasks to more meaningful pursuits in Quadrants I and II.

3. Review and Adjust Regularly:

- Weekly Review: Set aside time each week to review your Eisenhower Matrix. Assess how well you've been prioritizing your tasks and make any necessary adjustments. This regular review helps you stay on track and ensures that your actions align with your goals.

- Adjust as Needed: Life is dynamic, and your tasks and priorities may change over time. Be flexible and willing to adjust your matrix as needed. For example, if a new project arises, reallocate your time and energy to ensure that it fits within the appropriate quadrant.

4. Apply the Matrix in Different Contexts:

- Workplace Application: Use the Eisenhower Matrix to manage your work responsibilities. For example, when faced with multiple deadlines, categorize each task according to urgency and importance, and focus on completing the most critical tasks first.

- Personal Life Application

: The Eisenhower Matrix is equally valuable in managing personal responsibilities. For instance, you can use the matrix to prioritize self-care, family time, and personal development activities, ensuring that you maintain a balanced and fulfilling life.

Real-Life Example of the Eisenhower Matrix in Action

To illustrate the practical application of the Eisenhower Matrix, consider the following real-life example:

Case Study: Sarah, a Project Manager

Sarah is a project manager at a tech company, and she often feels overwhelmed by the demands of her job. She finds herself constantly putting out fires (Quadrant I) and responding to urgent requests (Quadrant III), leaving little time for long-term planning and personal development (Quadrant II). To regain control of her time and prioritize effectively, Sarah decides to use the Eisenhower Matrix.

- Step 1: Categorize Tasks: Sarah lists all of her current tasks and responsibilities. She identifies that many of her tasks, such as preparing for an upcoming project launch (Quadrant I), are both urgent and important. However, she also realizes that she's spending too much time on non-essential emails and meetings (Quadrant III) that don't contribute to her long-term goals.

- Step 2: Prioritize and Schedule: Sarah prioritizes her Quadrant I tasks and schedules dedicated time each day to address them. She also allocates time for Quadrant II activities, such as strategic planning and professional development, which she had previously neglected. To free up time, she delegates some Quadrant III tasks to her team and declines unnecessary meetings.

- Step 3: Eliminate Time-Wasters: Sarah identifies several Quadrant IV activities, such as checking social media during work hours, that are not contributing to her success. She decides to eliminate these distractions and replace them with more meaningful activities, such as taking short walks during breaks to recharge.

- Step 4: Regular Review: Sarah commits to reviewing her Eisenhower Matrix weekly to assess her progress and make any necessary adjustments. This regular review helps her stay focused on her priorities and ensures that she is making steady progress toward her goals.

As a result of using the Eisenhower Matrix, Sarah experiences a significant improvement in her productivity and work-life balance. She feels more in control of her time and is better able to focus on what truly matters, both in her career and personal life.

The Eisenhower Matrix is a powerful tool for prioritizing tasks and responsibilities, helping you manage your time effectively and focus on what truly matters. By categorizing tasks based on urgency and importance, you can allocate your time and energy to activities that align with your long-term goals and personal mission.

As you incorporate the Eisenhower Matrix into your daily life, you'll find that you become more intentional with your time, reduce stress, and achieve greater success and fulfillment. Remember to review and adjust your matrix regularly, and apply it across different contexts to ensure that you are consistently prioritizing the tasks that have the most significant impact on your life.

Techniques for Time Management and Prioritization

Time management and prioritization are essential skills for achieving success and maintaining balance in both your personal and professional life. With the demands of modern life, it's easy to feel overwhelmed by the sheer volume of tasks and responsibilities. Effective time management allows you to take control of your schedule, focus on what matters most, and make steady progress toward your goals. In this chapter, we will explore various techniques for time management and prioritization that can help you maximize your productivity and achieve greater fulfillment.

The Importance of Time Management and Prioritization

Before diving into specific techniques, it's important to understand why time management and prioritization are so crucial:

1. Increased Productivity:

- Effective time management enables you to get more done in less time. By prioritizing tasks and focusing on high-impact activities, you can maximize your productivity and achieve better results without overloading yourself.

2. Reduced Stress:

- When you manage your time well and prioritize effectively, you reduce the stress and anxiety that often come from feeling overwhelmed. A clear plan of action allows you to approach tasks with confidence and clarity, minimizing the chaos that can lead to burnout.

3. Enhanced Focus:

- Prioritization helps you concentrate on the tasks that matter most, eliminating distractions and unnecessary tasks. This focus ensures that your efforts are directed toward activities that align with your goals and values.

4. Better Work-Life Balance:

- Time management techniques can help you allocate time for both work and personal life, leading to a more balanced and fulfilling lifestyle. By setting boundaries and prioritizing self-care, you can avoid the pitfalls of overwork and maintain harmony in your life.

Techniques for Time Management

1. Time Blocking:

- What It Is: Time blocking is a technique where you schedule specific blocks of time for different tasks or activities throughout your day. Each block is dedicated to a single task, reducing the likelihood of multitasking and allowing for deep focus.

- How to Apply It:

- Start by identifying the most important tasks you need to complete.

- Assign specific time blocks for each task in your daily schedule, ensuring that you allocate enough time for completion.

- Stick to your time blocks as closely as possible, avoiding interruptions and distractions during each block.

- Include time blocks for breaks, self-care, and personal activities to ensure a balanced schedule.

- Benefits: Time blocking helps you structure your day, improve focus, and ensure that important tasks are completed without delay.

2. The Pomodoro Technique:

- What It Is: The Pomodoro Technique is a time management method that involves breaking your work into short, focused intervals called "Pomodoros," typically 25 minutes long, followed by a short break. After four Pomodoros, you take a longer break.

- How to Apply It:

- Choose a task you want to work on.

- Set a timer for 25 minutes and focus solely on that task until the timer goes off.

- Take a 5-minute break after each Pomodoro to recharge.

- After completing four Pomodoros, take a longer break (15-30 minutes) before starting the next round.

- Benefits: The Pomodoro Technique enhances focus, reduces mental fatigue, and increases productivity by encouraging regular breaks and sustained attention.

3. The Two-Minute Rule:

- What It Is: The Two-Minute Rule is a simple productivity hack that suggests if a task can be completed in two minutes or less, you should do it immediately rather than postponing it.

- How to Apply It:

- As you go through your task list, identify tasks that can be completed in two minutes or less.

- Complete these tasks immediately to clear them from your list and reduce clutter in your schedule.

- Use the rule to manage small tasks efficiently, preventing them from piling up and becoming overwhelming.

- Benefits: The Two-Minute Rule helps you manage small tasks quickly and efficiently, freeing up time for more important activities.

4. Batching Similar Tasks:

- What It Is: Task batching involves grouping similar tasks together and completing them in a single session. This approach reduces the cognitive load of switching between different types of tasks and increases efficiency.

- How to Apply It:

- Identify tasks that are similar in nature, such as responding to emails, making phone calls, or running errands.

- Schedule dedicated time blocks for each batch of similar tasks.

- Focus solely on completing one batch before moving on to the next, minimizing distractions and interruptions.

- Benefits: Batching similar tasks improves efficiency by allowing you to maintain focus on a specific type of activity and reduces the time lost in task-switching.

5. The 80/20 Rule (Pareto Principle):

- What It Is: The 80/20 Rule, also known as the Pareto Principle, suggests that 80% of your results come from 20% of your efforts. By identifying and focusing on the most impactful tasks, you can achieve more with less effort.

- How to Apply It:

- Analyze your tasks and identify the 20% that will have the greatest impact on your goals or results.

- Prioritize these high-impact tasks and allocate the majority of your time and resources to them.

- Minimize or delegate tasks that fall into the less impactful 80%, ensuring that your efforts are directed toward activities that produce the most significant outcomes.

- Benefits: The 80/20 Rule helps you focus on the tasks that truly matter, leading to more efficient and effective use of your time.

6. Setting Time Limits for Tasks:

- What It Is: Setting time limits involves assigning a specific amount of time to complete a task, which helps prevent tasks from expanding to fill the available time (a phenomenon known as Parkinson's Law).

- How to Apply It:

- Estimate how long each task should take to complete.

- Set a timer or deadline for each task and aim to complete it within the allotted time.

- Stay focused and avoid perfectionism, striving to complete tasks efficiently without unnecessary delays.

- Benefits: Setting time limits encourages efficiency, prevents tasks from dragging on longer than necessary, and helps you maintain momentum throughout the day.

Techniques for Prioritization

1. The Eisenhower Matrix:

- What It Is: The Eisenhower Matrix, discussed earlier in this chapter, is a prioritization tool that categorizes tasks into four quadrants based on their urgency and importance. It helps you prioritize tasks that have the most significant impact on your goals.

- How to Apply It:

- Categorize your tasks into the four quadrants: Urgent and Important, Not Urgent but Important, Urgent but Not Important, and Not Urgent and Not Important.

- Focus on completing tasks in the first two quadrants (Urgent and Important, Not Urgent but Important) while minimizing or delegating tasks in the other quadrants.

- Use the matrix regularly to review and adjust your priorities based on changing circumstances.

- Benefits: The Eisenhower Matrix helps you prioritize effectively, ensuring that your efforts are focused on tasks that align with your goals and values.

2. ABC Method:

- What It Is: The ABC Method is a simple prioritization technique that involves categorizing tasks into three groups: A (high priority), B (medium priority), and C (low priority). This method helps you focus on the most important tasks first.

- How to Apply It:

- Review your task list and assign each task a letter based on its priority level: A for high-priority tasks, B for medium-priority tasks, and C for low-priority tasks.

- Focus on completing A tasks first before moving on to B and C tasks.

- Reassess your priorities regularly and adjust the categorization as needed.

- Benefits: The ABC Method provides a straightforward way to prioritize tasks and ensures that the most critical tasks are completed first.

3. The Ivy Lee Method:

- What It Is: The Ivy Lee Method is a prioritization technique that involves identifying the six most important tasks to complete each day and focusing solely on those tasks until they are finished.

- How to Apply It:

- At the end of each workday, write down the six most important tasks you need to complete the next day.

- Rank these tasks in order of importance.

- Focus on completing the first task before moving on to the next, and continue working through the list until all six tasks are completed.

- Any unfinished tasks can be carried over to the next day's list.

- Benefits: The Ivy Lee Method provides a clear, focused approach to daily prioritization, helping you maintain momentum and achieve key objectives each day.

4. Eat That Frog Technique:

- What It Is: The "Eat That Frog" technique, popularized by Brian Tracy, involves tackling your most difficult or unpleasant task (the "frog") first thing in the morning. This technique ensures that you start your day with a sense of accomplishment and reduces procrastination.

- How to Apply It:

- Identify the most challenging or least appealing task on your to-do list—this is your "frog."

- Commit to completing this task first thing in the morning, before moving on to other tasks.

- Once the task is completed, enjoy the sense of relief and momentum that comes from getting the hardest task out of the way.

- Benefits: The Eat That Frog technique helps you overcome procrastination, build momentum, and start your day with a sense of accomplishment.

5. Rocks, Pebbles, and Sand Method

- What It Is: The Rocks, Pebbles, and Sand method is a metaphorical prioritization technique that encourages you to focus on "big rocks" (important tasks) before filling your time with "pebbles" (medium-priority tasks) and "sand" (low-priority tasks).

- How to Apply It:

- Identify your "big rocks," which are the most important tasks that must be completed.

- Schedule time to complete these big rocks first, ensuring that they receive the attention they deserve.

- Fill in the remaining time with "pebbles" (less important tasks) and "sand" (trivial tasks) as needed.

- Benefits: This method helps you prioritize the most important tasks and ensures that they are completed before less important activities take over your schedule.

6. MoSCoW Method:

- What It Is: The MoSCoW Method is a prioritization framework often used in project management that categorizes tasks into four groups: Must have, Should have, Could have, and Won't have.

- How to Apply It:

- Categorize your tasks based on their importance: Must have (essential tasks), Should have (important but not critical tasks), Could have (nice-to-have tasks), and Won't have (tasks that can be eliminated or postponed).

- Focus on completing "Must have" tasks first, followed by "Should have" tasks. Consider "Could have" tasks only if time permits, and eliminate or postpone "Won't have" tasks.

- Benefits: The MoSCoW Method helps you prioritize tasks effectively, ensuring that essential tasks are completed while minimizing time spent on less important activities.

Real-Life Example of Time Management and Prioritization

To illustrate the practical application of time management and prioritization techniques, consider the following real-life example:

Case Study: John, a Marketing Manager

John is a marketing manager at a mid-sized company. With multiple projects, meetings, and daily tasks competing for his attention, John often feels overwhelmed and struggles to prioritize his work effectively. To regain control of his time and improve his productivity, John decides to implement several time management and prioritization techniques.

- Time Blocking: John starts by using time blocking to structure his day. He schedules dedicated blocks of time for key tasks, such as content creation, team meetings, and strategic planning. This approach helps him focus on one task at a time and reduces distractions.

- The Pomodoro Technique: John applies the Pomodoro Technique for tasks that require deep concentration, such as writing reports or developing marketing strategies. By working in focused 25-minute intervals with short breaks, John maintains his energy and productivity throughout the day.

- The 80/20 Rule: John uses the 80/20 Rule to identify the tasks that have the most significant impact on his marketing campaigns. He prioritizes these high-impact tasks, such as optimizing ad spend and analyzing key performance metrics, ensuring that his efforts yield the best results.

- The Eisenhower Matrix: John regularly uses the Eisenhower Matrix to categorize and prioritize his tasks. By focusing on Quadrant I (Urgent and Important) and

Quadrant II (Not Urgent but Important) activities, John ensures that he is making progress on both immediate and long-term goals.

- Eat That Frog Technique: Each morning, John identifies his most challenging task for the day and completes it first. This approach helps him overcome procrastination and build momentum for the rest of the day.

As a result of implementing these techniques, John experiences a significant improvement in his time management and prioritization skills. He feels more in control of his schedule, reduces stress, and consistently meets his goals and deadlines.

Effective time management and prioritization are essential for achieving success and maintaining balance in your life. By applying techniques such as time blocking, the Pomodoro Technique, the Eisenhower Matrix, and the 80/20 Rule, you can take control of your schedule, focus on what matters most, and make steady progress toward your goals.

As you integrate these techniques into your daily routine, remember that time management and prioritization are ongoing processes that require regular reflection and adjustment. By consistently refining your approach, you can maximize your productivity, reduce stress, and create a more fulfilling and balanced life.

In the next chapter, we will explore strategies for balancing the various roles and responsibilities in your life, ensuring that you maintain harmony and fulfillment in all areas.

CHAPTER 04

BALANCING LIFE ROLES

Strategies for Managing Work, Family, and Personal Time Effectively

In today's fast-paced world, balancing the various roles and responsibilities we hold in life can be a challenging task. Whether it's managing a demanding career, nurturing relationships with family and friends, or finding time for personal growth and well-being, each role we play requires attention and energy. Achieving a harmonious balance between these roles is essential for leading a fulfilling life and maintaining overall well-being. In this chapter, we will explore strategies for effectively managing work, family, and personal time, allowing you to live a balanced and purposeful life.

Understanding the Importance of Balance

Before diving into specific strategies, it's important to understand why balancing life roles is so crucial:

1. Improved Well-Being:

- When you effectively balance your roles, you reduce stress and prevent burnout, leading to better physical and mental health. A balanced life fosters a sense of satisfaction and contentment, contributing to overall well-being.

2. Enhanced Relationships:

- Balancing work, family, and personal time allows you to nurture and maintain strong relationships with loved ones. Investing time and energy in relationships enhances emotional support and connection, which are vital for happiness.

3. Increased Productivity:

- When your life is balanced, you are more focused and productive in all areas. By managing your time effectively, you can achieve your professional goals while still making time for family and personal pursuits.

4. Greater Fulfillment:

- A balanced life enables you to pursue a variety of interests and passions, leading to a more fulfilling and enriched life. It allows you to grow in multiple dimensions—career, relationships, personal development—without sacrificing one for the other.

Strategies for Balancing Work, Family, and Personal Time

1. Set Clear Priorities:

- Identify Your Core Values: Begin by identifying your core values and what matters most to you in life. These values will serve as the foundation for setting priorities. For example, if family is a top priority, ensure that your schedule reflects this by allocating quality time for family activities.

- Rank Your Roles: List the various roles you play in life, such as employee, spouse, parent, friend, and individual. Rank these roles based on their importance and the amount of time and energy you want to dedicate to each. This ranking will help you allocate your resources more effectively and ensure that the most important roles receive the attention they deserve.

2. Create a Balanced Schedule:

- Use Time Blocking: Time blocking, discussed in the previous chapter, is an effective technique for creating a balanced schedule. Allocate specific blocks of time for work, family, and personal activities. Ensure that your schedule reflects your priorities and that each role is given appropriate time and attention.

- Include Buffer Time: Life is unpredictable, and unexpected events can disrupt even the most well-planned schedules. Include buffer time in your schedule to account for these interruptions. Buffer time allows you to handle unforeseen events without derailing your entire day.

3. Practice Effective Time Management:

- Prioritize Tasks: Use prioritization techniques, such as the Eisenhower Matrix, to manage your tasks effectively. Focus on completing high-priority tasks first, ensuring that important responsibilities in both work and personal life are addressed.

- Limit Multitasking: While multitasking might seem like a way to get more done, it often leads to decreased productivity and increased stress. Focus on one task at a time, whether it's a work project, spending time with family, or engaging in a personal hobby. Single-tasking allows you to be fully present in each moment, improving the quality of your work and interactions.

4. Set Boundaries:

- Define Work Hours: Clearly define your work hours and stick to them. Communicate these boundaries to your colleagues and clients to manage their expectations. Avoid bringing work home or checking work emails outside of designated work hours, allowing you to fully disconnect and focus on family and personal time.

- Protect Personal Time: Just as you set boundaries for work, protect your personal time by setting limits on social obligations, screen time, and other activities that may encroach on your time for self-care and personal growth. Prioritize activities that rejuvenate and fulfill you, such as exercise, reading, or pursuing a hobby.

5. Delegate and Share Responsibilities:

- Delegate at Work: If you find yourself overwhelmed with work tasks, consider delegating some responsibilities to colleagues or team members. Delegating allows you to focus on high-impact activities and reduces the likelihood of burnout.

- Share Family Responsibilities: At home, involve family members in sharing household responsibilities. Assign tasks based on each person's strengths and availability, creating a sense of teamwork and reducing the burden on any one individual. Sharing responsibilities also fosters a sense of cooperation and strengthens family bonds.

6. Make Time for Self-Care:

- Prioritize Physical Health: Your physical health is the foundation of your overall well-being. Make time for regular exercise, a balanced diet, and adequate sleep. Prioritizing your physical health not only improves your energy and focus but also enhances your ability to fulfill your roles effectively.

- Practice Mindfulness: Incorporate mindfulness practices, such as meditation, deep breathing, or journaling, into your daily routine. Mindfulness helps you stay grounded, reduces stress, and enhances your ability to manage the demands of daily life.

- Engage in Activities You Enjoy: Personal time is an opportunity to engage in activities that bring you joy and fulfillment. Whether it's pursuing a hobby, spending time in nature, or connecting with friends, make time for activities that nourish your soul and recharge your spirit.

7. Communicate Effectively:

- Discuss Expectations: Open communication is key to managing expectations in both your work and personal life. Discuss your needs and boundaries with your employer, colleagues, and family members. Clear communication helps prevent misunderstandings and ensures that everyone is on the same page.

- Ask for Support: Don't hesitate to ask for support when you need it. Whether it's seeking help from a coworker with a work task or asking a family member to assist with household chores, reaching out for support can lighten your load and reduce stress.

8. Regularly Reflect and Adjust:

- Conduct Regular Check-Ins: Set aside time each week or month to reflect on how well you are balancing your roles. Assess whether your current schedule and priorities are working for you, and make adjustments as needed. Regular reflection allows you to stay aligned with your goals and values, ensuring that you maintain a healthy balance over time.

- Be Flexible: Life is dynamic, and your roles and responsibilities may change over time. Be flexible and willing to adapt your approach as your circumstances evolve. For example, if you experience a major life event, such as the birth of a child or a career change, be prepared to adjust your schedule and priorities to accommodate these changes.

Real-Life Example of Balancing Life Roles

To illustrate how these strategies can be applied in real life, consider the following example:

Case Study: Maria, a Working Mother

Maria is a working mother of two young children. She juggles a demanding full-time job as a marketing director with her responsibilities as a parent and spouse. Maria values both her career and her family, but she often feels overwhelmed by the competing demands on her time. To achieve better balance, Maria decides to implement several strategies for managing her roles effectively.

- Setting Clear Priorities: Maria begins by identifying her core values, which include family, career, and personal growth. She ranks her roles based on these values, with her role as a mother and spouse taking top priority, followed by her career and personal development. This ranking helps her make decisions about how to allocate her time and energy.

- Creating a Balanced Schedule: Maria uses time blocking to create a balanced schedule that reflects her priorities. She blocks off time in the morning for family activities, such as preparing breakfast and spending time with her children before school. She dedicates the middle of the day to work tasks, ensuring that she remains focused and productive during work hours. In the evenings, Maria sets aside time for family dinner and personal activities, such as reading and exercise.

- Setting Boundaries: To protect her family and personal time, Maria establishes clear boundaries around her work hours. She communicates these boundaries to her colleagues, letting them know that she is unavailable after 6 p.m. and on weekends. By setting these boundaries, Maria ensures that she can fully disconnect from work and focus on her family and self-care.

- Delegating Responsibilities: At work, Maria delegates some of her tasks to her team members, allowing her to focus on high-priority projects. At home, she involves her spouse and children in sharing household responsibilities, such as cooking, cleaning, and managing schedules. This shared approach reduces Maria's workload and fosters a sense of teamwork within her family.

- Making Time for Self-Care: Maria prioritizes her physical and mental well-being by scheduling regular exercise sessions, practicing mindfulness, and engaging in activities she enjoys, such as gardening. By taking care of herself, Maria ensures that she has the energy and resilience needed to fulfill her roles effectively.

- Reflecting and Adjusting: Each week, Maria conducts a reflection session to assess how well she is balancing her roles. If she notices that one area of her life is receiving too much or too little attention, she adjusts her schedule accordingly. For example, if work demands increase during a busy season, Maria might temporarily adjust her work hours while ensuring that she still spends quality time with her family.

As a result of implementing these strategies, Maria experiences a significant improvement in her work-life balance. She feels more in control of her schedule, less stressed, and more fulfilled in both her career and family life. Maria's ability to balance her roles effectively allows her to lead a more harmonious and satisfying life.

Balancing work, family, and personal time is essential for leading a fulfilling and well-rounded life. By setting clear priorities, creating a balanced schedule, practicing effective time management, setting boundaries, and making time for self-care, you can manage your roles effectively and achieve greater harmony in your life.

Remember that balance is an ongoing process that requires regular reflection and adjustment. Be flexible and open to change, and don't hesitate to ask for support when needed. By implementing these strategies, you can create a life that reflects your values, fulfills your goals, and nurtures your well-being.

Think Win-Win

The Win-Win Paradigm: Understanding the Concept and Its Benefits

In the pursuit of personal and professional success, the mindset we adopt plays a critical role in shaping our interactions and outcomes. One of the most powerful paradigms for fostering positive relationships and achieving mutually beneficial results is the Win-Win paradigm. This concept, popularized by Stephen R. Covey in his seminal work The 7 Habits of Highly Effective People, emphasizes the importance of seeking solutions that benefit all parties involved. In this chapter, we will explore the concept of the Win-Win paradigm, its underlying principles, and the numerous benefits it offers in both personal and professional contexts.

Understanding the Win-Win Paradigm

The Win-Win paradigm is a mindset and approach to interactions that seeks outcomes where all parties involved gain something of value. It is based on the belief that life is not a zero-sum game—where one person's gain is another's loss—but rather an opportunity for collaboration and mutual benefit. The Win-Win mindset is built on the following core principles:

1. Mutual Benefit:

- Collaborative Approach: The Win-Win paradigm is rooted in the belief that it is possible to find solutions that satisfy the needs and interests of all parties. Instead of viewing negotiations or interactions as competitions where one side must win and the other must lose, the Win-Win approach seeks to create value for everyone involved. This collaborative mindset fosters an environment of cooperation rather than conflict.

- Shared Success: In a Win-Win scenario, success is not measured by how much one party gains at the expense of another, but by the extent to which all parties benefit. This principle encourages people to look beyond their own interests and consider the well-being and success of others, leading to outcomes that are sustainable and satisfying for everyone.

2. Abundance Mentality:

- Belief in Abundance: The Win-Win paradigm is closely tied to the concept of an abundance mentality. This mentality is based on the belief that there is enough success, wealth, and opportunity to go around, and that one person's gain does not diminish the potential for others to succeed. This stands in contrast to a scarcity mentality, which views resources as limited and promotes a zero-sum approach to interactions.

- Generosity and Openness: An abundance mentality encourages generosity, openness, and a willingness to share. When people adopt this mindset, they are more likely to collaborate, share ideas, and support others, knowing that mutual success is possible and that helping others does not diminish their own potential for success.

3. Integrity and Fairness:

- Commitment to Ethical Behavior: The Win-Win paradigm is grounded in integrity and fairness. It requires individuals to act honestly, transparently, and ethically in their interactions with others. By upholding these values, people build trust and credibility, which are essential for creating and sustaining Win-Win relationships.

- Equitable Solutions: Fairness is a key component of the Win-Win approach. It involves finding solutions that are equitable and just, ensuring that no party is taken advantage of or treated unfairly. This commitment to fairness fosters a sense of trust and respect, making it easier to reach agreements that benefit everyone.

4. Long-Term Relationships:

- Focus on Relationships: The Win-Win paradigm prioritizes long-term relationships over short-term gains. It recognizes that building strong, positive relationships is essential for achieving sustainable success. By seeking outcomes that benefit all parties, individuals can strengthen their relationships, leading to greater collaboration, loyalty, and trust over time.

- Mutual Respect: The Win-Win mindset is based on mutual respect and a genuine concern for the well-being of others. When individuals approach interactions with a focus on respect and empathy, they create an environment where all parties feel valued and understood, paving the way for more effective and harmonious relationships.

The Benefits of the Win-Win Paradigm

The Win-Win paradigm offers numerous benefits that can positively impact both personal and professional relationships. By adopting this mindset, individuals can achieve more meaningful and sustainable outcomes while fostering a culture of collaboration and mutual respect. Below are some of the key benefits of the Win-Win paradigm:

1. Enhanced Collaboration and Teamwork:

- Building Stronger Teams: The Win-Win approach encourages collaboration and teamwork by promoting a shared sense of purpose and mutual benefit. When team members are committed to finding solutions that work for everyone, they are more likely to support each other, share ideas, and work together effectively. This collaborative spirit enhances team cohesion, improves communication, and leads to better outcomes.

- Encouraging Innovation: A collaborative environment fosters creativity and innovation. When individuals feel that their contributions are valued and that their success is tied to the success of the group, they are more likely to think creatively and propose innovative solutions. The Win-Win paradigm creates a safe space for experimentation and risk-taking, leading to breakthroughs and improvements that benefit everyone.

2. Improved Negotiation Outcomes:

- Win-Win Negotiations: In negotiations, the Win-Win paradigm shifts the focus from competing for the largest share of the pie to expanding the pie so that all parties can gain more. This approach leads to more constructive and positive negotiations, where the emphasis is on finding mutually beneficial solutions rather than on winning at the expense of others. As a result, negotiations are more likely to end in agreements that are satisfying, sustainable, and beneficial to all involved.

- Building Long-Term Partnerships: Win-Win negotiations are particularly effective in building long-term partnerships. By prioritizing the interests of all parties and seeking equitable outcomes, individuals and organizations can establish trust and rapport, leading to stronger and more enduring relationships. These partnerships are more likely to thrive over time, as they are built on a foundation of mutual respect and shared success.

3. Increased Trust and Credibility:

- Building Trust: Trust is the cornerstone of any successful relationship, whether personal or professional. The Win-Win paradigm fosters trust by encouraging honesty, transparency, and ethical behavior. When individuals consistently act in ways that demonstrate their commitment to fairness and mutual benefit, they build credibility and earn the trust of others. This trust, in turn, makes it easier to collaborate, negotiate, and achieve shared goals.

- Enhancing Reputation: Individuals and organizations that consistently operate with a Win-Win mindset are often viewed as trustworthy, reliable, and fair. This positive reputation can open doors to new opportunities, attract partners and clients, and enhance one's standing in the community or industry. A reputation for fairness and integrity is a valuable asset that can contribute to long-term success and influence.

4. Sustainable and Satisfying Solutions:

- Long-Lasting Agreements: The solutions generated through the Win-Win paradigm are more likely to be sustainable and satisfying for all parties. Because these solutions are designed to meet the needs and interests of everyone involved, they are more likely to endure over time and require less renegotiation or conflict resolution. This stability is particularly valuable in business relationships, where long-term agreements can lead to ongoing success and collaboration.

- Greater Satisfaction: Individuals who engage in Win-Win interactions often experience greater satisfaction with the outcomes. Knowing that their needs have been met while also contributing to the success of others creates a sense of fulfillment and well-being. This satisfaction enhances the overall quality of life and contributes to more positive and harmonious relationships.

5. Reduced Conflict and Improved Conflict Resolution:

- Minimizing Conflict: The Win-Win paradigm reduces the likelihood of conflict by promoting cooperation and mutual understanding. When individuals approach interactions with the goal of finding solutions that work for everyone, they are less likely to engage in adversarial behavior or power struggles. This collaborative approach minimizes the potential for conflict and creates a more positive and constructive environment.

- Effective Conflict Resolution: When conflicts do arise, the Win-Win mindset provides a framework for resolving them effectively. By focusing on the underlying needs and interests of all parties, individuals can work together to find solutions that address the root causes of the conflict. This approach leads to more lasting and meaningful resolutions, reducing the need for ongoing disputes and fostering a more peaceful and cooperative atmosphere.

6. Empowerment and Personal Growth:

- Empowering Others: The Win-Win paradigm is empowering because it encourages individuals to take an active role in shaping their outcomes while also considering the needs of others. This empowerment fosters a sense of agency and confidence, as individuals realize that they have the ability to influence positive change and create value for themselves and others.

- Personal Growth: Adopting a Win-Win mindset also contributes to personal growth and development. By focusing on collaboration, empathy, and fairness, individuals can develop key interpersonal skills such as communication, negotiation, and emotional intelligence. These skills are invaluable in both personal and professional contexts and contribute to ongoing growth and success.

7. Positive Organizational Culture:

- Fostering a Collaborative Culture: In organizational settings, the Win-Win paradigm can help foster a culture of collaboration, trust, and mutual respect. When leaders and employees consistently operate with a Win-Win mindset, they create an environment where teamwork, innovation, and positive relationships thrive. This culture not only enhances employee satisfaction and engagement but also contributes to the overall success and resilience of the organization.

- Attracting and Retaining Talent: Organizations that embrace the Win-Win paradigm are often more attractive to top talent. Employees are drawn to workplaces where their contributions are valued, and where they can achieve success without compromising their values or well-being. By promoting a Win-Win culture, organizations can attract and retain talented individuals who are aligned with the company's mission and values.

Real-Life Examples of the Win-Win Paradigm

To illustrate the power and benefits of the Win-Win paradigm, consider the following real-life examples:

1. Business Negotiations:

- Example: The Starbucks and Conservation International Partnership

- In 1998, Starbucks formed a partnership with Conservation International (CI) to promote sustainable coffee farming practices. Instead of focusing solely on maximizing profits, Starbucks sought to create a Win-Win solution that would benefit both the company and coffee-growing communities. The partnership led to the development of ethical sourcing guidelines that improved the livelihoods of farmers while ensuring a steady supply of high-quality coffee for Starbucks. This Win-Win approach not only enhanced Starbucks' brand reputation but also contributed to environmental sustainability and community development.

2. Community Initiatives:

- Example: The Harlem Children's Zone

- The Harlem Children's Zone (HCZ) is a nonprofit organization that adopts a Win-Win approach to education and community development. Founded by Geoffrey Canada, HCZ aims to break the cycle of poverty by providing comprehensive support to children and families in Harlem. The organization's programs include education, health care, and social services, all designed to create a Win-Win outcome where both children and the broader community benefit. HCZ's success has led to improved educational outcomes, reduced crime rates, and greater community cohesion, demonstrating the power of the Win-Win paradigm in social change.

3. Workplace Collaboration:

- Example: Google's 20% Time Policy

- Google's 20% Time policy, which allows employees to spend 20% of their work time on projects of their choosing, is an example of the Win-Win paradigm in action. The policy encourages innovation and creativity by giving employees the freedom to pursue their passions and interests. In return, Google benefits from the innovative ideas and projects that emerge from this initiative. Many of Google's most successful products, including Gmail and Google Maps, were developed through the 20% Time policy, demonstrating how a Win-Win approach can drive innovation and business success.

The Win-Win paradigm is a powerful mindset that promotes collaboration, mutual benefit, and sustainable success in both personal and professional contexts. By understanding and embracing the principles of the Win-Win approach—mutual benefit, an abundance mentality, integrity and fairness, and long-term relationships—individuals and organizations can achieve outcomes that are satisfying and beneficial for all parties involved.

The benefits of the Win-Win paradigm are far-reaching, from enhanced collaboration and improved negotiation outcomes to increased trust, reduced conflict, and personal growth. By adopting a Win-Win mindset, you can create more positive and productive relationships, achieve sustainable success, and contribute to a culture of cooperation and mutual respect.

Techniques for Fostering Win-Win Relationships in Personal and Professional Settings

Building strong, mutually beneficial relationships is crucial for success and fulfillment in both personal and professional settings. The Win-Win paradigm is a powerful approach that encourages collaboration, empathy, and shared success, leading to outcomes where all parties benefit. In this chapter, we will explore practical techniques for fostering Win-Win relationships, helping you create positive and lasting connections with others.

Understanding the Foundations of Win-Win Relationships

Before diving into specific techniques, it's essential to understand the key principles that underpin Win-Win relationships:

1. Mutual Respect:

- Win-Win relationships are built on a foundation of mutual respect. This means valuing the perspectives, needs, and goals of others, even when they differ from your own. By showing respect, you create an environment where open communication and collaboration can thrive.

2. Empathy:

- Empathy is the ability to understand and share the feelings of others. In Win-Win relationships, empathy allows you to see situations from the other person's point of view, helping you find solutions that meet both your needs and theirs.

3. Collaboration:

- Collaboration involves working together to achieve a common goal. In a Win-Win relationship, both parties are committed to finding solutions that benefit everyone involved. This collaborative mindset fosters teamwork, innovation, and shared success.

4. Integrity:

- Integrity is the quality of being honest and having strong moral principles. In Win-Win relationships, integrity ensures that both parties act ethically and transparently, building trust and credibility.

Techniques for Fostering Win-Win Relationships

1. Active Listening:

- What It Is: Active listening is the practice of fully focusing on the speaker, understanding their message, and responding thoughtfully. It goes beyond simply hearing words; it involves being present, attentive, and engaged in the conversation.

- How to Apply It:

- Give Your Full Attention: When someone is speaking, give them your full attention. Avoid distractions such as checking your phone or thinking about your response while they are talking.

- Use Nonverbal Cues: Show that you are listening by using nonverbal cues such as nodding, maintaining eye contact, and leaning slightly forward. These signals convey that you are engaged and interested in what the other person is saying.

- Reflect and Clarify: Reflect on what the speaker has said by paraphrasing or summarizing their points. For example, you might say, "So, what I'm hearing is that you're concerned about the project deadline. Is that correct?" This technique helps ensure that you fully understand their perspective and shows that you value their input.

- Benefits: Active listening fosters trust, reduces misunderstandings, and creates a strong foundation for collaboration. By making others feel heard and understood, you lay the groundwork for a Win-Win relationship.

2. Communicate Openly and Honestly:

- What It Is: Open and honest communication involves expressing your thoughts, feelings, and needs clearly and respectfully. It also means being transparent about your intentions and goals.

- How to Apply It:

- Be Clear and Direct: When communicating, be clear and direct about what you want or need. Avoid vague language or beating around the bush. For example, instead of saying, "I'm not sure if I can meet that deadline," say, "I need an extra two days to complete the project to the best of my ability."

- Use "I" Statements: Use "I" statements to express your thoughts and feelings without placing blame. For example, say, "I feel concerned about the project timeline," instead of, "You're not managing the project well." This approach reduces defensiveness and encourages constructive dialogue.

- Be Honest About Your Needs: In a Win-Win relationship, it's essential to be honest about your needs and expectations. Clearly communicate what is important to you, and be open to discussing how those needs can be met in a way that also benefits the other party.

- Benefits: Open and honest communication builds trust and ensures that both parties are on the same page. It helps prevent misunderstandings and allows for more effective problem-solving, leading to mutually beneficial outcomes.

3. Seek to Understand Before Being Understood:

- What It Is: This principle, popularized by Stephen Covey, emphasizes the importance of understanding the other person's perspective before trying to communicate your own. It involves putting yourself in their shoes and seeing the situation from their point of view.

- How to Apply It:

- Ask Open-Ended Questions: Encourage the other person to share their thoughts and feelings by asking open-ended questions. For example, ask, "What are your thoughts on this proposal?" or "How do you feel about the direction of this project?"

- Listen Without Judgment: Listen to their response without interrupting or judging. Allow them to express their perspective fully before you offer your own.

- Validate Their Perspective: Acknowledge and validate their feelings, even if you don't agree with them. For example, you might say, "I can see why you're feeling frustrated, given the challenges we've faced."

- Benefits: By seeking to understand the other person first, you demonstrate empathy and respect. This approach fosters trust and cooperation, making it easier to find solutions that work for both parties.

4. Focus on Interests, Not Positions:

- What It Is: In negotiations and problem-solving, focusing on interests means looking beyond the specific positions or demands each party holds and understanding the underlying needs and motivations driving those positions. This approach allows for more creative and flexible solutions.

- How to Apply It:

- Identify Underlying Interests: Ask questions to uncover the underlying interests behind the other person's position. For example, if a colleague insists on a specific deadline, ask why that deadline is important to them. They might reveal that it's tied to another project's timeline or a client's expectations.

- Explore Common Interests: Identify any common interests or goals that both parties share. For example, both you and your colleague might have a shared interest in delivering high-quality work or maintaining a good client relationship.

- Brainstorm Win-Win Solutions: Once you understand the underlying interests, brainstorm solutions that address those interests while also meeting your own needs.

For example, you might agree on a deadline extension that still allows for client satisfaction while giving your team more time to produce quality work.

- Benefits: Focusing on interests rather than positions opens up more possibilities for collaboration and compromise. It helps avoid deadlock and enables both parties to find creative solutions that satisfy their needs.

5. Practice Flexibility and Adaptability:

- What It Is: Flexibility and adaptability involve being open to change and willing to adjust your approach when necessary. In a Win-Win relationship, this means being willing to consider alternative solutions and make compromises that benefit both parties.

- How to Apply It:

- Stay Open-Minded: Approach interactions with an open mind, ready to explore different options and perspectives. Avoid getting too attached to a single solution or outcome.

- Be Willing to Compromise: Recognize that a Win-Win solution often requires compromise. Be willing to give up certain demands or adjust your expectations to find a solution that works for both parties.

- Adapt to Changing Circumstances: Life is dynamic, and circumstances can change. Be willing to adapt your approach as new information or situations arise. For example, if a project scope changes, be flexible in renegotiating deadlines or responsibilities.

- Benefits: Flexibility and adaptability help you navigate complex situations and find solutions that are fair and beneficial for all involved. This approach fosters a positive and cooperative relationship, even in the face of challenges.

6. Build Trust Through Consistency:

- What It Is: Trust is built through consistent behavior over time. In a Win-Win relationship, this means consistently acting with integrity, keeping your promises, and following through on commitments.

- How to Apply It:

- Keep Your Word: If you make a commitment, follow through on it. Whether it's meeting a deadline, attending a meeting, or delivering on a promise, consistency in your actions builds trust.

- Be Reliable: Be someone others can rely on. This means showing up on time, being prepared, and delivering quality work consistently.

- Communicate Transparently: If you encounter challenges that prevent you from fulfilling a commitment, communicate openly and transparently. Let the other person know as soon as possible and work together to find a solution.

- Benefits: Consistency builds trust, which is the foundation of any strong relationship. When others know they can count on you, they are more likely to engage in collaborative and mutually beneficial interactions.

7. Celebrate Shared Successes:

- What It Is: Celebrating shared successes involves recognizing and appreciating the achievements and contributions of everyone involved in a Win-Win relationship. It reinforces positive behavior and strengthens the bond between parties.

- How to Apply It:

- Acknowledge Contributions: Take the time to acknowledge and thank others for their contributions to a successful outcome. Whether it's a team project at work or a collaborative effort at home, recognition fosters goodwill and strengthens relationships.

- Celebrate Milestones Together: Celebrate key milestones and achievements together, whether it's through a formal celebration, a casual gathering, or simply sharing words of appreciation.

- Express Gratitude: Regularly express gratitude for the positive aspects of your relationships. Let others know that you value their partnership and are grateful for the collaboration.

- Benefits: Celebrating shared successes strengthens relationships and reinforces the collaborative spirit of the Win-Win paradigm. It creates a positive and supportive environment where everyone feels valued and motivated to continue working together.

Real-Life Examples of Fostering Win-Win Relationships

To illustrate how these techniques can be applied in real life, consider the following examples:

1. Professional Collaboration:

- Example: Cross-Departmental Project at a Tech Company

- Sarah, a project manager at a tech company, is tasked with leading a cross-departmental project that involves both the engineering and marketing teams. To foster a Win-Win relationship between the two teams, Sarah begins by practicing active listening and open communication. She holds a kickoff meeting where both teams are encouraged to share their perspectives, goals, and concerns. Sarah seeks to understand the interests of each team, such as the engineering team's focus on technical excellence and the marketing team's need for timely product launches. By focusing on common interests and practicing flexibility, Sarah helps the teams brainstorm solutions that meet both technical and marketing requirements. Throughout the project, Sarah builds trust by consistently following through on commitments and celebrating shared successes, such as meeting key milestones. As a result, the project is completed successfully, and both teams feel satisfied with the outcome, having achieved their goals collaboratively.

2. Personal Relationships:

- Example: Resolving a Disagreement in a Marriage

- John and Maria, a married couple, find themselves in a disagreement about how to spend their upcoming vacation. John wants to go on an adventure trip, while Maria prefers a relaxing beach getaway. To resolve the disagreement, they decide to practice the Win-Win approach. They begin by seeking to understand each other's perspective—John shares that he's been feeling restless and wants to experience something new, while Maria explains that she's been stressed at work and needs time to unwind. By focusing on their underlying interests (John's need for excitement and Maria's need for relaxation), they brainstorm a solution that satisfies both of them: a trip that includes a few days of adventure followed by a few days of relaxation. By being flexible and communicating openly, John and Maria reach a Win-Win solution that strengthens their relationship and ensures that both of their needs are met.

Fostering Win-Win relationships is a powerful way to create positive, collaborative, and mutually beneficial connections in both personal and professional settings. By practicing techniques such as active listening, open communication, empathy, and flexibility, you can build trust, strengthen relationships, and achieve outcomes that benefit everyone involved.

The principles of the Win-Win paradigm—mutual respect, collaboration, integrity, and shared success—serve as a foundation for these techniques, guiding your interactions and helping you create lasting and meaningful relationships. As you apply these strategies in your daily life, you will find that Win-Win relationships not only lead to better outcomes but also contribute to greater fulfillment, satisfaction, and harmony in all areas of your life.

Negotiation and Conflict Resolution: Practical Tips for Creating Mutually Beneficial Solutions

Negotiation and conflict resolution are integral parts of both personal and professional life. Whether it's negotiating a contract at work, resolving a disagreement with a colleague, or managing conflicts in personal relationships, the ability to find mutually beneficial solutions is crucial for maintaining positive relationships and achieving successful outcomes. The Win-Win paradigm offers a powerful approach to negotiation and conflict resolution, emphasizing collaboration, empathy, and shared success. In this chapter, we will explore practical tips and strategies for applying the Win-Win approach to create solutions that benefit all parties involved.

Understanding the Win-Win Approach to Negotiation and Conflict Resolution

The Win-Win approach to negotiation and conflict resolution is based on the principle that both parties can achieve their goals without one side having to lose. It moves away from adversarial, zero-sum thinking and instead focuses on collaboration and mutual benefit. The core elements of the Win-Win approach include:

1. Collaboration Over Competition:

- Instead of viewing negotiation as a battle to be won, the Win-Win approach sees it as a collaborative process where both parties work together to find a solution that meets their respective needs.

2. Focus on Interests, Not Positions:

- The Win-Win approach emphasizes the importance of understanding the underlying interests and needs of both parties, rather than focusing solely on their stated positions or demands.

3. Creative Problem-Solving:

- Finding a Win-Win solution often requires creativity and a willingness to explore alternative options that satisfy both parties' interests.

4. Mutual Respect and Empathy:

- The Win-Win approach is grounded in mutual respect and empathy, recognizing the importance of considering the other party's perspective and treating them with fairness and dignity.

Practical Tips for Creating Mutually Beneficial Solutions

1. Prepare Thoroughly:

- Understand Your Goals: Before entering a negotiation or conflict resolution process, take the time to clearly define your goals and priorities. What are the most important outcomes you want to achieve? What are your non-negotiables? Understanding your objectives will help you stay focused and avoid unnecessary concessions.

- Research the Other Party's Interests: In addition to understanding your own goals, research the interests and needs of the other party. What are their priorities? What challenges or constraints might they be facing? The more you understand the other party's perspective, the better positioned you'll be to find common ground and propose solutions that work for both sides.

- Anticipate Challenges: Consider potential challenges or objections that may arise during the negotiation or conflict resolution process. Think about how you can address these challenges constructively and propose alternatives that keep the conversation moving forward.

2. Start with a Positive Attitude:

- Set a Collaborative Tone: Begin the negotiation or conflict resolution process with a positive and collaborative attitude. Express your willingness to work together to find a solution that benefits both parties. This sets the tone for a productive and respectful discussion.

- Avoid Adversarial Language: Use language that is inclusive and constructive rather than adversarial. For example, instead of saying, "I need you to agree to this," you might say, "Let's explore how we can find a solution that works for both of us."

3. Focus on Interests, Not Positions:

- Ask Open-Ended Questions: To uncover the other party's underlying interests, ask open-ended questions that encourage them to share their perspective. For example, ask, "What are your main concerns with this proposal?" or "What are the key outcomes you're hoping to achieve?"

- Listen Actively: Pay close attention to the other party's responses and try to understand the motivations behind their positions. Reflect back on what you've heard to ensure you've accurately captured their interests. For example, you might say, "It sounds like your main priority is ensuring the project stays on budget. Is that correct?"

- Identify Shared Interests: Look for common interests or goals that both parties share. These shared interests can serve as a foundation for building a mutually beneficial solution. For example, if both parties are interested in maintaining a long-term partnership, you can frame the negotiation around finding a solution that strengthens that relationship.

4. Generate Multiple Options:

- Brainstorm Together: Once you've identified the interests of both parties, engage in a brainstorming session to generate multiple options for resolving the issue. Encourage creativity and avoid judging ideas too quickly. The goal is to explore a range of possibilities that could meet both parties' needs.

- Evaluate Options Collaboratively: After generating several options, evaluate them together based on how well they address the interests of both parties. Consider the pros and cons of each option and discuss potential adjustments that could make a solution more acceptable to both sides.

- Aim for Win-Win Solutions: Look for solutions that provide mutual benefit and avoid compromising on key interests. A Win-Win solution should leave both parties feeling satisfied with the outcome and confident in the fairness of the agreement.

5. Be Willing to Compromise:

- Know Your Priorities: While the goal is to find a Win-Win solution, it's important to recognize that compromise may be necessary. Be clear about your priorities and be willing to make concessions on less important issues to achieve a mutually beneficial outcome.

- Seek Balanced Trade-Offs: When making concessions, aim for balanced trade-offs where both parties give up something of lesser importance in exchange for gaining something of greater value. This approach helps ensure that both sides feel they've gained something meaningful from the negotiation.

- Maintain Flexibility: Flexibility is key to successful negotiation and conflict resolution. Be open to adjusting your approach or considering alternative solutions if it helps move the conversation forward and achieve a positive outcome.

6. Build and Maintain Trust:

- Act with Integrity: Trust is essential for successful negotiation and conflict resolution. Act with integrity by being honest, transparent, and consistent in your actions. Avoid making promises you can't keep or using deceptive tactics.

- Follow Through on Commitments: If you reach an agreement, follow through on your commitments in a timely and reliable manner. Demonstrating your reliability builds trust and strengthens the relationship for future interactions.

- Communicate Openly: Keep the lines of communication open throughout the process. If any issues or concerns arise after an agreement is reached, address them promptly and constructively. Open communication helps prevent misunderstandings and ensures that both parties remain satisfied with the outcome.

7. Manage Emotions Effectively:

- Stay Calm and Composed: Negotiations and conflict resolution can be emotionally charged, but it's important to stay calm and composed. If you feel yourself becoming frustrated or defensive, take a moment to breathe and refocus on the goals of the conversation.

- Acknowledge Emotions: Recognize and acknowledge the emotions of both yourself and the other party. For example, if the other party seems upset, you might say, "I can see that this issue is really important to you, and I want to make sure we find a solution that addresses your concerns."

- De-Escalate Tensions: If tensions rise, take steps to de-escalate the situation. This might involve taking a short break, shifting the focus to a less contentious issue, or using humor to lighten the mood. The goal is to keep the conversation productive and prevent emotions from derailing the process.

8. Create a Collaborative Agreement:

- Summarize Key Points: As you approach a resolution, summarize the key points of the agreement to ensure that both parties have a clear understanding of the terms. This helps prevent any misunderstandings and ensures that everyone is on the same page.

- Document the Agreement: If appropriate, document the agreement in writing. This can be particularly important in professional settings where formal contracts or agreements are needed. A written agreement provides a clear reference point and helps ensure that both parties adhere to the terms.

- Celebrate the Agreement: Once an agreement is reached, take a moment to acknowledge and celebrate the successful resolution. Express appreciation for the other party's collaboration and commitment to finding a mutually beneficial solution.

9. Plan for the Future:

- Discuss Implementation: After reaching an agreement, discuss how the terms will be implemented. Clarify roles, responsibilities, and timelines to ensure that both parties know what to expect moving forward.

- Monitor Progress: Keep track of how the agreement is being implemented and check in with the other party to ensure that everything is proceeding as planned. If any issues arise, address them promptly and collaboratively.

- Build Long-Term Relationships: Use the successful resolution of the negotiation or conflict as a foundation for building a stronger long-term relationship. Continue to apply the principles of the Win-Win approach in future interactions to maintain a positive and collaborative dynamic.

Real-Life Examples of Win-Win Negotiation and Conflict Resolution

To illustrate how these tips can be applied in real-life scenarios, consider the following examples:

1. Negotiating a Salary Increase:

- Example: Emma, a skilled software engineer, feels that her salary is not commensurate with her contributions to the company. She prepares thoroughly by researching industry salary standards, understanding her own value, and considering the company's financial situation. During the negotiation, Emma adopts a positive attitude and focuses on her contributions to the company's success. She listens to her manager's perspective and learns that while the company values her work, they are facing budget constraints. Emma proposes a Win-Win solution: a phased salary increase tied to specific performance milestones, combined with additional professional development opportunities. By being flexible and focusing on mutual benefit, Emma secures a salary increase that aligns with her goals while addressing the company's concerns.

2. Resolving a Workplace Conflict:

- Example: Two colleagues,

Mark and Lisa, have a conflict over the direction of a joint project. Mark wants to prioritize speed to meet a tight deadline, while Lisa is concerned about maintaining high-quality standards. To resolve the conflict, their manager facilitates a Win-Win discussion. They begin by identifying the underlying interests: Mark's focus on meeting client expectations and Lisa's commitment to delivering quality work. Together, they brainstorm solutions and agree to allocate additional resources to the project, allowing them to meet the deadline without compromising quality. By focusing on shared interests and being open to creative solutions, Mark and Lisa resolve the conflict and strengthen their working relationship.

The Win-Win approach to negotiation and conflict resolution offers a powerful framework for achieving mutually beneficial outcomes in both personal and professional settings. By focusing on collaboration, empathy, and shared success, you can navigate challenging situations with confidence and build stronger, more positive relationships.

The practical tips and strategies outlined in this chapter—preparing thoroughly, focusing on interests, generating multiple options, being willing to compromise, building trust, managing emotions, and creating collaborative agreements—provide a roadmap for applying the Win-Win approach in your daily life. As you incorporate these techniques into your interactions, you'll find that you can achieve better outcomes, reduce conflict, and create lasting, mutually beneficial relationships.

CHAPTER 05

SEEK FIRST TO UNDERSTAND, THEN TO BE UNDERSTOOD

Effective Communication: The Art of Active Listening and Empathy

Communication is the cornerstone of all human interactions, whether in personal relationships, professional environments, or social settings. However, communication is not just about expressing your thoughts and ideas—it's equally about understanding others. Stephen R. Covey's principle, "Seek First to Understand, Then to Be Understood," emphasizes the importance of truly listening to others before making your own point. This chapter will delve into two essential components of effective communication: active listening and empathy. By mastering these skills, you can improve your relationships, build trust, and foster a deeper connection with others.

Understanding Active Listening

Active listening is more than just hearing words; it's a conscious effort to understand the message being conveyed, both verbally and nonverbally. It involves fully concentrating, understanding, responding, and then remembering what is being said. Active listening is a skill that requires practice, patience, and a willingness to genuinely engage with the speaker.

The Components of Active Listening

1. Full Attention:

- Focus on the Speaker: Active listening begins with giving the speaker your undivided attention. This means setting aside distractions, such as your phone or computer, and focusing entirely on the person speaking. It's important to be present in the moment, mentally and physically.

- Maintain Eye Contact: Eye contact is a powerful way to show that you are engaged and interested in what the speaker is saying. It helps build a connection and reassures the speaker that you are listening.

2. Nonverbal Cues:

- Body Language: Your body language speaks volumes during a conversation. Nod occasionally to show understanding, and lean slightly forward to convey interest.

Avoid crossing your arms or looking away, as these can be perceived as disinterest or defensiveness.

- Facial Expressions: Use appropriate facial expressions that reflect the emotions being conveyed by the speaker. If they are sharing something joyful, smile; if they are discussing something serious, maintain a neutral or concerned expression.

3. Reflective Listening:

- Paraphrasing: Reflective listening involves paraphrasing what the speaker has said to confirm your understanding. For example, you might say, "So, you're saying that you're feeling overwhelmed with your current workload?" This technique not only clarifies the message but also shows the speaker that you are actively engaged.

- Summarizing: At the end of a conversation or after the speaker has made a significant point, summarize what you've heard. This helps ensure that you've captured the main ideas and allows the speaker to correct any misunderstandings.

4. Avoiding Interruptions:

- Let the Speaker Finish: Interruptions can disrupt the flow of conversation and make the speaker feel unheard or disrespected. Practice patience by allowing the speaker to finish their thoughts before responding.

- Hold Back Judgments: It's easy to jump to conclusions or form judgments while someone is speaking, but doing so can prevent you from truly understanding their perspective. Approach the conversation with an open mind and listen fully before offering your opinions.

5. Asking Open-Ended Questions:

- Encourage Elaboration: Open-ended questions invite the speaker to expand on their thoughts and feelings. For example, instead of asking, "Did you like the meeting?" ask, "What were your thoughts on the meeting?" This type of question encourages deeper discussion and provides more insight into the speaker's perspective.

6. Providing Feedback:

- Offer Thoughtful Responses: After the speaker has finished, provide feedback that shows you've been listening and that you value their input. This could be in the form of asking follow-up questions, offering support, or sharing your own thoughts on the topic.

The Benefits of Active Listening

1. Builds Trust and Respect:

- When people feel heard and understood, they are more likely to trust and respect you. Active listening creates a safe space for open and honest communication, which is essential for building strong relationships.

2. Enhances Understanding:

- Active listening helps you gain a deeper understanding of the speaker's perspective, needs, and emotions. This understanding is crucial for resolving conflicts, making informed decisions, and fostering collaboration.

3. Reduces Misunderstandings:

- By focusing fully on the speaker and confirming your understanding through reflective listening, you can significantly reduce the chances of misunderstandings and miscommunication.

4. Strengthens Relationships:

- Whether in personal or professional settings, relationships are strengthened when both parties feel heard and valued. Active listening is a key ingredient in maintaining healthy, positive interactions.

Understanding Empathy

Empathy is the ability to understand and share the feelings of another person. It goes beyond mere sympathy (feeling sorry for someone) and involves putting yourself in their shoes, experiencing their emotions, and understanding their perspective. Empathy is a critical component of emotional intelligence and plays a vital role in effective communication and relationship building.

The Components of Empathy

1. Perspective-Taking:

- See the World Through Their Eyes: Perspective-taking involves imagining how the other person perceives the situation. This requires you to step outside of your own experiences and biases and consider how the situation might look and feel from the other person's point of view.

- Avoid Assumptions: Instead of assuming you know how the other person feels, ask questions and listen to their explanations. For example, "Can you help me understand how this situation is affecting you?"

2. Emotional Resonance:

- Feel What They Feel: Emotional resonance means connecting with the emotions the other person is experiencing. If they are sad, you allow yourself to feel their sadness; if they are excited, you share in their excitement. This emotional connection is key to showing genuine empathy.

- Acknowledge Their Emotions: Validate the other person's feelings by acknowledging them openly. For instance, "It sounds like you're really frustrated with how things turned out. I can understand why you'd feel that way."

3. Compassionate Action:

- Respond with Care: Empathy often leads to compassionate action, where you offer support, help, or comfort to the other person. This could be as simple as offering a listening ear, providing a solution, or just being present for them during difficult times.

- Avoid Fixing: While it's natural to want to fix the problem, sometimes the best way to show empathy is simply to listen and be there for the person. Ask them what they need rather than assuming a solution.

4. Nonjudgmental Support:

- Offer a Safe Space: Empathy requires creating a space where the other person feels safe to express their emotions without fear of judgment. This involves listening without criticizing, blaming, or offering unsolicited advice.

- Respect Their Experience: Everyone's experiences and emotions are unique. Even if you don't fully understand why someone feels a certain way, respect their right to their emotions and offer support without judgment.

The Benefits of Empathy

1. Deepens Connections:

- Empathy allows you to connect with others on a deeper emotional level. This connection fosters trust, intimacy, and mutual understanding, which are essential for building strong, meaningful relationships.

2. Enhances Conflict Resolution:

- When conflicts arise, empathy helps you understand the other person's perspective and emotions, making it easier to find common ground and resolve disagreements amicably.

3. Promotes Emotional Healing:

- Empathy provides emotional support to those who are struggling, helping them feel less alone and more understood. This can be incredibly healing, especially in times of distress or difficulty.

4. Improves Teamwork and Collaboration:

- In professional settings, empathy enhances teamwork and collaboration by promoting a culture of understanding, respect, and mutual support. When team members empathize with each other, they are more likely to work together effectively and achieve shared goals.

Practical Steps to Develop Active Listening and Empathy

1. Practice Mindfulness:

- Be Present: Mindfulness is the practice of being fully present in the moment, which is crucial for both active listening and empathy. Before entering a conversation, take a moment to clear your mind of distractions and focus entirely on the interaction at hand.

- Observe Your Thoughts and Emotions: During the conversation, be aware of your own thoughts and emotions. If you notice yourself becoming distracted or judgmental, gently bring your focus back to the speaker.

2. Engage in Empathy Exercises:

- Perspective-Taking Exercises: Regularly practice putting yourself in others' shoes by imagining how they might feel in different situations. You can do this in everyday interactions or by reflecting on past experiences where empathy was needed.

- Empathy Journaling: Keep a journal where you reflect on interactions that required empathy. Write about how you felt, how the other person might have felt, and what you could have done to better understand their perspective.

3. Cultivate Emotional Intelligence:

- Develop Self-Awareness: Emotional intelligence starts with self-awareness—understanding your own emotions and how they influence your behavior. By developing self-awareness, you become better equipped to recognize and manage your emotions during interactions with others.

- Practice Emotional Regulation: Learn to manage your emotions, especially in challenging situations. Emotional regulation allows you to stay calm and composed, which is essential for both active listening and empathy.

4. Seek Feedback:

- Ask for Input: Seek feedback from trusted friends, colleagues, or mentors about your listening and empathy skills. Ask them how well they feel heard and understood in your conversations and where you might improve.

- Reflect on Feedback: Reflect on the feedback you receive and use it to make adjustments in your communication style. Continuous improvement is key to becoming a better listener and more empathetic communicator.

5. Observe and Learn from Others:

- Identify Role Models: Identify individuals who excel at active listening and empathy, whether they are people in your life, public figures, or fictional characters. Observe how they interact with others and what makes their communication effective.

- Incorporate Positive Traits: Incorporate the positive traits you observe into your own communication style. For example, if you notice that a colleague is particularly good at asking open-ended questions, try to adopt that habit in your own conversations.

Real-Life Examples of Active Listening and Empathy

To illustrate how active listening and empathy can be applied in real-life situations, consider the following examples:

1. Personal Relationship:

- Example: Sarah and James, a married couple, are discussing a recent argument. Instead of defending his position, James practices active listening by giving Sarah his full attention and paraphrasing her concerns. He says, "I hear that you felt hurt when I didn't consult you before making that decision." By actively listening, James helps Sarah feel understood, which opens the door for a more constructive conversation. He then demonstrates empathy by acknowledging her feelings and apologizing for his oversight. This approach not only resolves the conflict but also strengthens their emotional connection.

2. Professional Setting:

- Example: During a team meeting, Lisa, a project manager, notices that one of her team members, Tom, seems disengaged. After the meeting, she pulls Tom aside and practices active listening by asking open-ended questions about how he's feeling. Tom shares that he's been overwhelmed with his workload. Lisa responds with empathy, saying, "I can see how the workload might feel overwhelming. Let's work together to find a solution that eases some of that burden." By actively listening and empathizing with Tom, Lisa not only addresses the issue but also builds trust and rapport with her team member.

Active listening and empathy are essential skills for effective communication and building strong, meaningful relationships. By mastering these skills, you can foster deeper connections with others, resolve conflicts more effectively, and create an environment of trust and mutual respect.

The art of active listening involves giving your full attention, using nonverbal cues, reflecting and paraphrasing, avoiding interruptions, asking open-ended questions, and providing thoughtful feedback. Empathy, on the other hand, requires perspective-taking, emotional resonance, compassionate action, and nonjudgmental support.

As you practice and develop these skills, you will find that your interactions with others become more positive, productive, and fulfilling. By seeking first to understand, then to be understood, you can enhance your communication, strengthen your relationships, and create a more empathetic and connected world.

Techniques for Improving Communication and Understanding Others

Effective communication is not just about expressing your own thoughts and ideas; it's equally about understanding others. When you prioritize understanding the perspectives, emotions, and intentions of those you interact with, you foster stronger relationships, reduce misunderstandings, and create an environment of trust and cooperation. In this chapter, we will explore a range of techniques for improving communication and enhancing your ability to understand others, whether in personal relationships, professional settings, or social interactions.

1. Practice Active Listening

Active listening is the foundation of effective communication. It involves fully concentrating on what the other person is saying, both verbally and nonverbally, without allowing distractions or preconceived notions to interfere.

Techniques for Active Listening:

- Eliminate Distractions: Before engaging in a conversation, remove any potential distractions. This might mean putting away your phone, closing your laptop, or choosing a quiet place to talk. Being fully present signals to the other person that they have your full attention.

- Maintain Eye Contact: Eye contact is a powerful way to show that you are engaged and interested in what the speaker is saying. It helps build trust and demonstrates that you value the conversation.

- Use Nonverbal Cues: Nonverbal communication, such as nodding, smiling, or leaning slightly forward, shows that you are actively engaged in the conversation. These cues encourage the speaker to continue and provide reassurance that you are listening.

- Paraphrase and Reflect: To ensure that you have understood the speaker correctly, paraphrase or summarize what they've said. For example, you might say, "So, you're saying that you're feeling frustrated with the current situation, is that right?" This technique not only clarifies the message but also shows the speaker that you are fully engaged.

- Avoid Interrupting: Let the speaker finish their thoughts before you respond. Interrupting can disrupt the flow of conversation and may lead to misunderstandings. By allowing the speaker to complete their message, you ensure that you fully understand their perspective.

2. Ask Open-Ended Questions

Open-ended questions are designed to encourage a full, meaningful answer, rather than a simple "yes" or "no." They are a powerful tool for deepening your understanding of others.

Techniques for Asking Open-Ended Questions:

- Encourage Elaboration: Instead of asking, "Did you like the presentation?" which can be answered with a simple "yes" or "no," try asking, "What did you think of the presentation?" This type of question invites the other person to share more details and provides a richer understanding of their perspective.

- Explore Emotions: When appropriate, ask questions that explore the other person's feelings or emotions. For example, "How did that situation make you feel?" or "What concerns do you have about this decision?" Understanding emotions can provide deeper insights into the other person's viewpoint.

- Probe for Clarification: If something is unclear, don't hesitate to ask for clarification. For instance, "Can you explain a bit more about what you meant by that?" or "I'm not sure I understand—could you elaborate?" Clarifying questions help prevent misunderstandings and ensure that both parties are on the same page.

- Avoid Leading Questions: Leading questions suggest a particular answer and can bias the response. Instead of asking, "Don't you think this approach is better?" ask, "What are your thoughts on this approach?" This encourages a more honest and open response.

3. Develop Empathy

Empathy is the ability to understand and share the feelings of another person. It is a critical component of effective communication and helps build stronger, more meaningful connections.

Techniques for Developing Empathy:

- Put Yourself in Their Shoes: Try to imagine how the other person might be feeling in their situation. Consider their background, experiences, and emotions. This perspective-taking can help you better understand their reactions and needs.

- Acknowledge Their Emotions: When someone expresses their feelings, acknowledge them openly. For example, "It sounds like you're really frustrated right now, and I can understand why." Acknowledging emotions helps the other person feel validated and understood.

- Use Empathetic Language: Use language that conveys empathy and understanding. Phrases like "I can see how that would be difficult" or "That must have been really challenging for you" show that you are tuned into the other person's emotional state.

- Be Nonjudgmental: Avoid passing judgment on the other person's feelings or reactions. Empathy requires accepting the other person's emotions as valid, even if you don't agree with them. This nonjudgmental approach creates a safe space for open communication.

4. Clarify and Confirm Understanding

Miscommunication often arises when assumptions are made, or when people believe they understand each other without verifying that understanding. Clarifying and confirming what has been communicated ensures that both parties are aligned.

Techniques for Clarifying and Confirming Understanding:

- Restate Key Points: After a conversation, especially one involving complex or important information, restate the key points to ensure clarity. For example, "Just to make sure we're on the same page, you're suggesting that we proceed with option A, correct?"

- Ask for Confirmation: After summarizing the conversation, ask the other person to confirm that your understanding is correct. This can be as simple as, "Is that right?" or "Did I miss anything?"

- Use "I" Statements: When seeking clarification, use "I" statements to express your need for understanding without sounding accusatory. For example, "I'm not sure I'm following—could you explain that part again?"

- Encourage Feedback: Invite the other person to provide feedback on your understanding. Ask, "Do you think that covers everything?" or "Is there anything else you'd like to add?" This allows them to correct any misunderstandings or provide additional context.

5. Adapt Your Communication Style

Effective communication requires flexibility and the ability to adapt your style to suit the needs of the situation and the person you are communicating with.

Techniques for Adapting Your Communication Style:

- Consider the Audience: Tailor your communication style to the needs and preferences of the person you're speaking with. For example, some people prefer direct, to-the-point communication, while others may appreciate more context and detail.

- Adjust Your Tone: Your tone of voice can significantly impact how your message is received. In situations requiring sensitivity, use a softer, more empathetic tone. In professional settings, a more assertive and confident tone may be appropriate.

- Match the Medium to the Message: Choose the appropriate medium for your communication. For example, complex or sensitive issues may be better discussed in person or via video call, while straightforward updates can be communicated via email or text.

- Be Aware of Cultural Differences: Cultural differences can influence communication styles and expectations. Be mindful of these differences and adjust your approach as needed. For example, in some cultures, indirect communication and avoiding confrontation are valued, while in others, directness and assertiveness are preferred.

6. Be Patient and Give Time

Effective communication often requires patience, especially when dealing with complex issues or emotions. Giving time for the other person to express themselves fully without feeling rushed can lead to better understanding and more meaningful exchanges.

Techniques for Practicing Patience:

- Allow Pauses: Don't rush to fill silences in a conversation. Pauses give the other person time to think and formulate their thoughts, leading to more considered responses.

- Avoid Interrupting: Let the other person finish their thoughts before you respond. Interrupting can disrupt their train of thought and may lead to incomplete communication.

- Show Willingness to Listen: Sometimes, people need time to open up. Show that you're willing to listen by being patient and giving them the space to speak when they're ready.

- Respect Different Paces: Everyone communicates at their own pace. Some people need more time to articulate their thoughts, while others may process information more slowly. Respect these differences and avoid rushing the conversation.

7. Recognize and Manage Nonverbal Communication

Nonverbal communication, including body language, facial expressions, and gestures, plays a significant role in how messages are conveyed and interpreted. Being aware of and managing your nonverbal signals can enhance your communication effectiveness.

Techniques for Managing Nonverbal Communication:

- Be Aware of Your Body Language: Your posture, gestures, and facial expressions can communicate a lot about your feelings and attitudes. For example, crossing your arms might be perceived as defensive, while an open posture can signal openness and receptivity.

- Observe the Other Person's Nonverbal Cues: Pay attention to the nonverbal signals of the person you're communicating with. Are they making eye contact? Do they seem tense or relaxed? These cues can provide insight into how they are feeling and how they are interpreting the conversation.

- Align Verbal and Nonverbal Messages: Ensure that your nonverbal signals match your verbal messages. For example, if you're expressing empathy, your tone of voice, facial expression, and body language should all convey warmth and understanding.

- Use Gestures Purposefully: Gestures can enhance your communication when used appropriately. For example, using hand movements to emphasize key points can make your message more engaging and memorable.

8. Practice Reflective Thinking

Reflective thinking involves taking the time to reflect on your interactions and communication practices. By considering what went well and what could be improved, you can continuously enhance your communication skills.

Techniques for Reflective Thinking:

- Reflect After Conversations: After significant conversations, take a few moments to reflect on how the interaction went. Ask yourself questions like, "Did I fully understand the other person's perspective?" or "Was there anything I could have communicated more clearly?"

- Keep a Communication Journal: Consider keeping a journal where you record your thoughts and reflections on your communication experiences. This can help you identify patterns, strengths, and areas for improvement.

- Seek Feedback: Ask others for feedback on your communication style. This could be a trusted colleague, friend, or mentor. Their insights can provide valuable perspectives and help you improve.

- Set Goals for Improvement: Based on your reflections and feedback, set specific goals for improving your communication skills. For example, you might aim to practice active listening more consistently or to be more mindful of your nonverbal communication.

Real-Life Examples of Improving Communication and Understanding Others

To illustrate how these techniques can be applied in real-life situations, consider the following examples:

1. Workplace Communication:

- Example: Jane, a team leader, noticed that some of her team members were hesitant to speak up during meetings. To improve communication, she started practicing active listening by asking open-ended questions and allowing more time for responses. She also adjusted her communication style by using more inclusive language and being mindful of cultural differences within her team. As a result, her team members felt more comfortable sharing their ideas, leading to more collaborative and productive meetings.

2. Personal Relationships:

- Example: Tom and Emily, a couple, were having recurring arguments about household responsibilities. To improve their communication, they decided to set aside time for a weekly check-in where they could discuss any concerns. During these check-ins, they practiced empathy by acknowledging each other's feelings and using "I" statements to express their needs. By being patient and giving each other time to speak without interruption, they were able to better understand each other's perspectives and find solutions that worked for both of them.

Improving communication and understanding others is an ongoing process that requires intention, practice, and patience. By incorporating techniques such as active listening, asking open-ended questions, developing empathy, clarifying and confirming understanding, adapting your communication style, practicing patience, managing nonverbal communication, and engaging in reflective thinking, you can enhance your ability to connect with others and build stronger, more meaningful relationships.

These skills are essential not only for effective communication but also for fostering a deeper understanding and connection with those around you. As you continue to practice and refine these techniques, you will find that your interactions become more positive, productive, and fulfilling, leading to greater success in both your personal and professional life.

Building Strong Relationships: Strategies for Gaining Trust and Fostering Collaboration

Strong relationships are the foundation of success in both personal and professional settings. Trust and collaboration are key components of these relationships, allowing individuals to work together effectively, overcome challenges, and achieve shared goals. Building trust and fostering collaboration requires intentional effort, effective communication, and a commitment to mutual respect. In this chapter, we will explore strategies for gaining trust and fostering collaboration, providing you with practical tools to strengthen your relationships and enhance your ability to work effectively with others.

Understanding the Importance of Trust in Relationships

Trust is the cornerstone of any strong relationship. Without trust, communication breaks down, collaboration falters, and relationships become strained. Trust is built over time through consistent actions, transparency, and reliability. It requires both parties to demonstrate honesty, integrity, and respect for one another.

The Benefits of Trust in Relationships

1. Enhanced Collaboration:

- Trust fosters an environment where individuals feel safe to share ideas, take risks, and collaborate openly. When trust is present, people are more likely to work together effectively, contribute their best efforts, and support one another.

2. Increased Resilience:

- Trust enables relationships to withstand challenges and setbacks. When trust is strong, individuals are more likely to give each other the benefit of the doubt, communicate openly during difficult times, and work together to find solutions.

3. Improved Communication:

- Trust encourages honest and transparent communication. When people trust each other, they are more willing to express their thoughts, feelings, and concerns without fear of judgment or retribution.

4. Greater Satisfaction:

- Trust leads to more satisfying and fulfilling relationships. When trust is present, individuals feel valued, respected, and understood, contributing to a positive and supportive environment.

Strategies for Gaining Trust

1. Demonstrate Consistency and Reliability:

- Keep Your Promises: One of the most effective ways to build trust is to consistently follow through on your commitments. Whether it's meeting deadlines, attending meetings, or delivering on promises, reliability is key to establishing trust. If you promise to do something, make sure you do it.

- Be Punctual: Punctuality is a simple but powerful way to demonstrate reliability. Showing up on time for meetings, appointments, and events signals that you respect the other person's time and that you can be counted on.

- Be Dependable: When others know they can rely on you, trust naturally follows. This means being available when needed, offering support during challenging times, and consistently delivering quality work.

2. Communicate Openly and Transparently:

- Be Honest: Honesty is a fundamental component of trust. Be truthful in your communications, even when the truth is difficult to share. If you've made a mistake, own up to it and take responsibility. Honesty builds credibility and shows that you have integrity.

- Share Information: Transparency involves sharing relevant information openly and without withholding important details. Keeping others informed about decisions, plans, and developments fosters trust and ensures that everyone is on the same page.

- Avoid Hidden Agendas: Trust is undermined when people feel that there are hidden agendas or ulterior motives at play. Be clear about your intentions and avoid manipulating situations to serve your own interests. A transparent approach fosters a sense of security and trust.

3. Show Empathy and Understanding:

- Listen Actively: Listening actively to others is a powerful way to build trust. It shows that you value their perspective and are willing to take the time to understand their concerns and needs. When people feel heard, they are more likely to trust you.

- Acknowledge Their Feelings: Empathy involves recognizing and validating the emotions of others. Acknowledge their feelings, even if you don't fully agree with them. For example, you might say, "I can see that you're frustrated, and I understand why this situation is challenging for you."

- Be Compassionate: Show compassion in your interactions by offering support and understanding. Whether it's providing a listening ear or offering help during difficult times, compassionate actions build trust and strengthen relationships.

4. Practice Fairness and Integrity:

- Be Fair: Fairness involves treating others equitably and without favoritism. Make decisions based on merit and be consistent in your actions. When people see that you are fair, they are more likely to trust your judgment and leadership.

- Act with Integrity: Integrity means doing the right thing, even when it's difficult or inconvenient. It involves standing by your principles and being consistent in your actions and words. Acting with integrity builds trust because it shows that you are guided by strong ethical values.

- Avoid Gossip and Negative Talk: Refrain from engaging in gossip or speaking negatively about others behind their backs. This behavior can quickly erode trust. Instead, focus on positive and constructive communication that uplifts and supports others.

5. Be Open to Feedback and Willing to Change:

- Seek Feedback: Actively seek feedback from others about how you can improve your communication and interactions. This shows that you value their input and are committed to personal growth. When people see that you are open to feedback, they are more likely to trust you.

- Acknowledge Mistakes: When you make a mistake, acknowledge it openly and take steps to correct it. Apologizing when necessary and demonstrating a willingness to learn from your errors builds trust and shows that you are accountable.

- Adapt and Improve: Use the feedback you receive to make positive changes in your behavior and interactions. Continuous improvement demonstrates that you are committed to building and maintaining trust over time.

Fostering Collaboration

Collaboration is the process of working together to achieve a common goal. In any relationship, whether personal or professional, fostering collaboration involves creating an environment where everyone feels valued, respected, and empowered to contribute.

The Benefits of Collaboration

1. Innovation and Creativity:

    - Collaboration brings together diverse perspectives, skills, and ideas, leading to more innovative and creative solutions. When people work together, they can build on each other's strengths and generate ideas that might not have emerged in isolation.

2. Improved Problem-Solving:

    - Collaborative problem-solving involves leveraging the collective knowledge and expertise of a group to address challenges. By working together, individuals can identify more effective solutions and make better decisions.

3. Shared Responsibility:

    - Collaboration fosters a sense of shared responsibility and ownership. When everyone is involved in the process, they are more likely to be committed to the outcome and work towards its success.

4. Stronger Relationships:

    - Collaborative efforts strengthen relationships by building trust, respect, and mutual support. When people collaborate successfully, they develop a deeper connection and a greater sense of camaraderie.

Strategies for Fostering Collaboration

1. Create a Culture of Inclusivity:

- Encourage Participation: Foster an environment where everyone feels encouraged to participate and share their ideas. Make it clear that all contributions are valued, regardless of the individual's role or position. Encourage quieter or less confident members to share their thoughts, ensuring that everyone has a voice.

- Embrace Diversity: Diversity in thought, experience, and background enriches collaboration. Embrace and celebrate the diverse perspectives within your team or group, and recognize that these differences can lead to more innovative and well-rounded solutions.

- Avoid Groupthink: While consensus is important, it's also crucial to avoid groupthink, where everyone agrees without critically evaluating ideas. Encourage open dialogue and respectful disagreement to ensure that all viewpoints are considered.

2. Set Clear Goals and Expectations:

- Define Common Goals: Clearly define the goals and objectives of the collaboration. Make sure that everyone understands the purpose and desired outcomes. When people have a shared vision, they are more motivated to work together towards that goal.

- Clarify Roles and Responsibilities: Clearly outline each person's role and responsibilities within the collaboration. This ensures that everyone knows what is expected of them and how they can contribute to the success of the project.

- Establish Ground Rules: Set ground rules for how the group will work together, communicate, and make decisions. This might include guidelines for meeting conduct, decision-making processes, and conflict resolution. Clear expectations help prevent misunderstandings and ensure smooth collaboration.

3. Facilitate Open Communication:

- Foster Transparency: Encourage open and transparent communication within the group. Share information freely and keep everyone informed about progress, challenges, and changes. Transparency builds trust and ensures that everyone is on the same page.

- Promote Active Listening: Encourage active listening during discussions. This means giving full attention to the speaker, avoiding interruptions, and asking clarifying questions. Active listening ensures that everyone's ideas are heard and understood.

- Use Collaborative Tools: Leverage collaborative tools such as shared documents, project management software, and communication platforms to facilitate seamless collaboration. These tools help keep everyone organized, informed, and connected.

4. Encourage Collaboration Over Competition:

- Promote a Team Mentality: Emphasize the importance of working together as a team rather than competing against one another. Highlight that success is achieved through collective effort, and recognize the contributions of the entire group.

- Celebrate Group Achievements: Celebrate successes as a group, recognizing the contributions of all members. This fosters a sense of shared accomplishment and reinforces the value of collaboration.

- Address Competitive Behavior: If competitive behavior arises, address it promptly and redirect the focus back to collaboration. Reinforce the idea that collaboration leads to better outcomes for everyone involved.

5. Provide Support and Resources:

- Offer Guidance: Provide the necessary support and guidance to ensure that the collaboration is successful. This might include offering mentorship, providing access to resources, or helping to resolve conflicts.

- Ensure Access to Resources: Make sure that the team has access to the resources they need to succeed, whether it's information, tools, or funding. Removing barriers to collaboration helps the group focus on achieving their goals.

- Be Available: Make yourself available to answer questions, provide feedback, and offer support when needed. Your involvement and availability demonstrate your commitment to the collaboration and help keep the project on track.

6. Build Trust Within the Group:

- Encourage Team-Building Activities: Organize team-building activities that help group members get to know each other better and build trust. These activities can range from formal workshops to informal social events.

- Foster a Safe Environment: Create a safe environment where team members feel comfortable expressing their ideas, taking risks, and admitting mistakes. When people feel safe, they are more likely to collaborate openly and honestly.

- Demonstrate Trust in Others: Show trust in others by delegating responsibilities and allowing team members to take ownership of their tasks. Trusting others encourages them to step up and contribute their best efforts.

Real-Life Examples of Gaining Trust and Fostering Collaboration

To illustrate how these strategies can be applied in real-life situations, consider the following examples:

1. Workplace Collaboration:

- Example: Maria is leading a cross-functional project at her company, which involves team members from marketing, engineering, and customer support. To foster collaboration, she begins by setting clear goals and defining each team member's role. Maria encourages open communication by holding regular check-ins where team members can share updates and discuss challenges. She also creates a culture of inclusivity by ensuring that all voices are heard during meetings and by embracing the diverse perspectives within the team. When the project faces a setback, Maria addresses it transparently, involving the team in brainstorming solutions. By building trust and fostering collaboration, Maria leads the team to successfully complete the project, with all members feeling valued and invested in the outcome.

2. Community Collaboration:

- Example: In a small town, local leaders are working together to revitalize the downtown area. To gain trust and foster collaboration among residents, they begin by holding town hall meetings where community members can voice their ideas and concerns. The leaders demonstrate transparency by sharing detailed plans and progress reports, and by being honest about challenges. They foster a culture of collaboration by organizing volunteer groups, encouraging residents to participate in the revitalization efforts. Trust is built through consistent communication, responsiveness to feedback, and recognition of the community's contributions. As a result, the revitalization project becomes a shared success, with strong community support and involvement.

Building strong relationships through trust and collaboration is essential for achieving success in both personal and professional settings. By demonstrating consistency, communicating openly, showing empathy, practicing fairness, and being open to feedback, you can gain the trust of others and create a solid foundation for collaboration.

Fostering collaboration involves creating an inclusive culture, setting clear goals, facilitating open communication, encouraging teamwork, providing support, and building trust within the group. When trust and collaboration are present, individuals are more likely to work together effectively, generate innovative solutions, and achieve shared goals.

As you apply these strategies in your interactions, you will find that your relationships become stronger, more positive, and more productive. Trust and collaboration not only lead to better outcomes but also create a sense of connection and fulfillment that enriches all aspects of your life.

In the next chapter, we will explore the concept of synergy in teamwork and collaboration, and how combining the strengths and perspectives of individuals can lead to greater collective success.

CHAPTER 06

SYNERGIZE

The Power of Teamwork: Understanding Synergy and Its Benefits

In a world that often emphasizes individual achievement, the concept of synergy reminds us of the extraordinary power of teamwork. Synergy occurs when the combined efforts of a group produce a result that is greater than the sum of their individual contributions. It is the essence of collaboration and the driving force behind some of the most successful teams and organizations. Understanding and harnessing the power of synergy can lead to remarkable outcomes, not only in professional settings but in all areas of life. This chapter delves into the concept of synergy, explores its benefits, and illustrates how it can transform ordinary teamwork into extraordinary results.

What Is Synergy?

Synergy is derived from the Greek word "synergos," meaning "working together." It refers to the phenomenon where the collaborative efforts of a group create an outcome that is superior to what could have been achieved individually. Synergy is more than just cooperation—it is the result of creative collaboration, where different perspectives, talents, and ideas come together to generate innovative solutions and achieve common goals.

The Components of Synergy

1. Diversity of Perspectives:

   - Synergy thrives on diversity. When people with different backgrounds, experiences, and viewpoints come together, they bring unique perspectives to the table. This diversity fuels creativity and innovation, allowing the group to explore a wider range of possibilities and solutions.

2. Complementary Strengths:

   - In a synergistic team, each member's strengths complement those of the others. Rather than everyone trying to do the same thing, team members leverage their individual skills and talents to contribute in ways that enhance the overall effectiveness of the group.

3. Shared Goals:

   - Synergy is most powerful when everyone is aligned with a common purpose or goal. Shared goals create a sense of unity and focus, directing the collective energy of the group toward achieving a desired outcome.

4. Open Communication:

- Effective communication is the backbone of synergy. Open, honest, and transparent communication ensures that ideas flow freely, misunderstandings are minimized, and everyone is on the same page. This level of communication allows the team to work together seamlessly.

5. Mutual Respect and Trust:

- For synergy to occur, there must be a foundation of mutual respect and trust among team members. When individuals feel valued and trusted, they are more likely to contribute their best efforts and collaborate openly with others.

The Stages of Synergy Development

1. Forming:

- In the forming stage, team members come together and begin to understand each other's strengths, weaknesses, and perspectives. This stage involves building relationships, establishing trust, and setting the groundwork for collaboration.

2. Storming:

- The storming stage is characterized by differences in opinions, approaches, and ideas. While conflicts may arise, this stage is crucial for surfacing diverse viewpoints and beginning the process of integrating them into a cohesive approach.

3. Norming:

- In the norming stage, the team starts to find common ground and align on shared goals. Roles and responsibilities become clearer, and the team develops norms and standards for how they will work together.

4. Performing:

- In the performing stage, synergy is fully realized. The team works collaboratively, leveraging each member's strengths, and achieving results that exceed individual capabilities. Communication flows smoothly, and the group is highly productive.

5. Adjourning:

- The adjourning stage occurs when the team has achieved its goals and is ready to disband or move on to new challenges. This stage involves reflecting on the experience, celebrating successes, and learning from the collaboration.

The Benefits of Synergy

Synergy offers a wide range of benefits that can enhance both individual and group performance. Understanding these benefits can help you recognize the value of fostering synergy in your own teams and collaborations.

1. Enhanced Creativity and Innovation:

- Diverse Ideas Lead to Breakthroughs: When team members bring different perspectives and ideas to the table, the possibilities for creative solutions multiply. Synergy allows for the cross-pollination of ideas, leading to innovative approaches that might not have been discovered through individual effort alone.

- Encourages Experimentation: In a synergistic environment, team members feel safe to experiment, take risks, and explore new ideas. This freedom to innovate often results in breakthroughs that can propel the team or organization forward.

2. Improved Problem-Solving:

- Leveraging Collective Intelligence: Synergy allows teams to tap into the collective intelligence of the group. When faced with complex problems, the team can draw on the knowledge, skills, and experiences of all members, leading to more effective and comprehensive solutions.

- Faster Resolution of Challenges: The collaborative nature of synergy means that challenges are addressed more quickly and efficiently. Team members work together to identify and implement solutions, reducing the time it takes to overcome obstacles.

3. Greater Efficiency and Productivity:

- Maximizing Resources: Synergy allows teams to maximize the use of their resources, including time, talent, and materials. By working together, team members can streamline processes, reduce redundancies, and accomplish tasks more efficiently.

- Increased Output: The combined efforts of a synergistic team often lead to increased output. Whether it's completing projects ahead of schedule, exceeding performance targets, or delivering higher-quality results, synergy boosts productivity.

4. Stronger Relationships and Team Cohesion:

- Building Trust and Respect: Synergy fosters an environment of mutual trust and respect. As team members collaborate and achieve success together, their relationships strengthen, leading to greater cohesion and camaraderie.

- Creating a Positive Team Culture: A synergistic team culture is characterized by positivity, support, and collaboration. This culture not only enhances team dynamics but also attracts and retains top talent, as people are drawn to environments where they feel valued and empowered.

5. Higher Levels of Engagement and Satisfaction:

- Empowerment and Ownership: In a synergistic team, individuals feel empowered to contribute their ideas and take ownership of their work. This sense of ownership leads to higher levels of engagement and satisfaction, as team members feel that their contributions are making a meaningful impact.

- Shared Success: Achieving success as a team is inherently rewarding. When team members work together to accomplish something significant, the sense of shared achievement boosts morale and reinforces the value of collaboration.

6. Better Decision-Making:

- Informed Choices: Synergy improves decision-making by ensuring that decisions are informed by a wide range of perspectives and insights. This holistic approach reduces the likelihood of errors and increases the chances of making sound, effective decisions.

- Balanced Approach: A synergistic team considers both the short-term and long-term implications of their decisions, as well as the needs and interests of all stakeholders. This balanced approach leads to more sustainable and successful outcomes.

7. Greater Adaptability and Resilience:

- Flexibility in the Face of Change: Synergistic teams are better equipped to adapt to changes and uncertainties. The collaborative nature of synergy allows teams to pivot quickly, reallocate resources, and develop creative solutions to new challenges.

- Resilience Through Support: The strong relationships and trust built through synergy provide a support network that helps teams navigate difficult times. When challenges arise, team members can rely on each other for encouragement and assistance, enhancing the team's overall resilience.

Real-Life Examples of Synergy in Action

To illustrate the power of synergy, consider the following real-life examples where teamwork and collaboration led to extraordinary results:

1. The Apollo 11 Mission:

- The successful landing of Apollo 11 on the moon in 1969 was a prime example of synergy in action. Thousands of scientists, engineers, and technicians from various disciplines worked together to achieve a goal that seemed impossible. The diversity of expertise, combined with a shared vision and seamless communication, resulted in one of the most significant achievements in human history. The success of the Apollo 11 mission demonstrated the power of synergy to overcome complex challenges and accomplish extraordinary feats.

2. The Manhattan Project:

- During World War II, the Manhattan Project brought together some of the brightest minds in science, including physicists, chemists, and engineers, to develop the first nuclear weapons. The collaboration between these experts, along with the pooling of resources and knowledge from multiple countries, led to the development of the atomic bomb. While the ethical implications of the project are widely debated, the Manhattan Project is a stark example of how synergy can drive rapid innovation and solve complex problems through the combined efforts of a diverse team.

3. Google's Cross-Functional Teams:

- Google is known for its use of cross-functional teams to drive innovation and problem-solving. By bringing together individuals from different departments—such as engineering, design, marketing, and product management—Google leverages the diverse perspectives and skills of its employees to create innovative products and solutions. The synergy within these teams has led to the development of some of Google's most successful products, such as Gmail, Google Maps, and the Android operating system.

4. The Success of Pixar Animation Studios:

- Pixar's success as a leading animation studio is largely attributed to its culture of collaboration and synergy. At Pixar, the creative process is highly collaborative, with directors, writers, animators, and technical experts working together to bring stories to life. The studio's "braintrust" meetings, where teams come together to provide candid feedback and ideas, are a key component of Pixar's synergy. This collaborative approach has resulted in a string of critically acclaimed and commercially successful films, including Toy Story, Finding Nemo, and Inside Out.

How to Foster Synergy in Teams

Creating synergy within a team requires intentional effort and leadership. Here are some strategies to foster synergy and harness its benefits:

1. Encourage Open Communication

- Create an environment where team members feel comfortable sharing their ideas, opinions, and feedback. Encourage open dialogue and active listening to ensure that all voices are heard. Transparent communication is the foundation of synergy, as it allows ideas to flow freely and fosters mutual understanding.

2. Leverage Individual Strengths:

- Recognize and utilize the unique strengths and talents of each team member. Assign roles and responsibilities that align with individual skills and expertise, allowing everyone to contribute in the most meaningful way. When team members feel that their strengths are being valued and utilized, they are more likely to engage fully and contribute to the team's success.

3. Promote Diversity and Inclusion:

- Embrace diversity within the team, including diversity of thought, experience, and background. A diverse team brings a wider range of perspectives and ideas, which can lead to more innovative and effective solutions. Ensure that all team members feel included and valued, and create opportunities for everyone to contribute.

4. Set Clear and Shared Goals:

- Establish clear goals that the entire team is working toward. Ensure that everyone understands the objectives and how their contributions align with the team's overall mission. Shared goals create a sense of unity and purpose, driving the team to work together effectively.

5. Encourage Collaboration Over Competition:

- Foster a culture where collaboration is prioritized over competition. Emphasize the importance of working together to achieve shared success, rather than competing for individual recognition. Recognize and celebrate team achievements, reinforcing the value of collective effort.

6. Facilitate Team-Building Activities:

- Organize team-building activities that strengthen relationships, build trust, and enhance collaboration. These activities can range from formal workshops to informal social events. Team-building helps create a sense of camaraderie and ensures that team members are comfortable working together.

7. Be a Supportive Leader:

- As a leader, support your team by providing guidance, resources, and encouragement. Be available to address challenges, mediate conflicts, and offer constructive feedback. A supportive leader fosters a positive team environment where synergy can thrive.

Synergy is the driving force behind extraordinary teamwork. When individuals come together, combining their diverse strengths, perspectives, and ideas, they can achieve results that far exceed what they could accomplish alone. Understanding the power of synergy and its benefits— enhanced creativity, improved problem-solving, greater efficiency, stronger relationships, higher engagement, better decision-making, and increased adaptability—can transform the way you approach collaboration in both personal and professional settings.

By fostering open communication, leveraging individual strengths, promoting diversity, setting clear goals, encouraging collaboration, facilitating team-building, and providing supportive leadership, you can create a synergistic environment that empowers your team to achieve remarkable success. As you embrace synergy in your interactions, you will discover the true potential of teamwork and the incredible outcomes that can be achieved when people work together toward a common goal.

Techniques for Creating Effective and Collaborative Teams

Building an effective and collaborative team is essential for achieving success in any organization or group. Collaboration harnesses the collective strengths, skills, and perspectives of team members, leading to better problem-solving, innovation, and productivity. However, creating such a team requires intentional effort, strategic planning, and a commitment to fostering a culture of trust and open communication. In this chapter, we will explore various techniques for creating teams that not only work well together but also achieve outstanding results through synergy.

1. Define Clear Goals and Objectives

One of the most critical factors in creating an effective and collaborative team is establishing clear goals and objectives. Without a shared understanding of what the team is working toward, collaboration can become unfocused and ineffective.

Techniques for Defining Clear Goals:

- Set SMART Goals: Ensure that team goals are Specific, Measurable, Achievable, Relevant, and Time-bound

(SMART). This clarity helps team members understand exactly what is expected of them and provides a framework for measuring progress.

- Align Goals with the Team's Purpose: Make sure that the goals align with the broader mission and purpose of the team or organization. When team members see how their work contributes to the bigger picture, they are more motivated to collaborate and achieve results.

- Communicate Goals Effectively: Clearly communicate the goals to all team members, ensuring that everyone is on the same page. Regularly revisit these goals during team meetings to keep everyone focused and aligned.

- Involve the Team in Goal Setting: Involving the team in the goal-setting process can increase buy-in and commitment. When team members have a say in defining the goals, they are more likely to feel ownership and responsibility for achieving them.

2. Build Trust and Mutual Respect

Trust and mutual respect are the foundation of any collaborative team. Without trust, team members may be reluctant to share ideas, take risks, or rely on one another, which can hinder collaboration.

Techniques for Building Trust:

- Lead by Example: As a leader or team member, demonstrate trustworthiness through your actions. Be consistent, reliable, and honest in your interactions. Show that you trust others by delegating responsibilities and giving them the autonomy to complete their tasks.

- Encourage Open Communication: Foster an environment where team members feel comfortable sharing their thoughts, concerns, and feedback. Open communication builds trust by ensuring that everyone's voice is heard and valued.

- Practice Active Listening: Show respect for your team members by actively listening to their ideas and concerns. Acknowledge their contributions and respond thoughtfully. This approach not only builds trust but also strengthens relationships within the team.

- Address Conflicts Constructively: When conflicts arise, address them promptly and constructively. Encourage open discussion and focus on finding solutions rather than assigning blame. Resolving conflicts fairly and transparently reinforces trust among team members.

3. Foster a Culture of Collaboration

Creating a culture of collaboration means prioritizing teamwork over individual achievement. It involves creating an environment where collaboration is valued, encouraged, and rewarded.

Techniques for Fostering Collaboration:

- Promote a Team Mentality: Emphasize the importance of teamwork in achieving the team's goals. Reinforce the idea that success is a collective effort and that everyone's contributions are essential.

- Facilitate Regular Team Meetings: Hold regular team meetings to discuss progress, share ideas, and address challenges. These meetings provide an opportunity for team members to collaborate, align on priorities, and stay connected.

- Encourage Knowledge Sharing: Create opportunities for team members to share their expertise and knowledge with one another. This could involve presentations, workshops, or informal knowledge-sharing sessions. When team members learn from each other, they build a deeper understanding and appreciation of each other's strengths.

- Celebrate Collaborative Successes: Recognize and celebrate successes that result from collaboration. Acknowledge the contributions of all team members and highlight how working together led to achieving the team's goals. This recognition reinforces the value of collaboration.

4. Leverage Individual Strengths and Diversity

Every team member brings unique skills, experiences, and perspectives to the table. Effective teams leverage these individual strengths to enhance collaboration and achieve better outcomes.

Techniques for Leveraging Strengths and Diversity:

- Identify and Utilize Strengths: Take the time to understand the strengths and talents of each team member. Assign roles and responsibilities that align with these strengths, allowing everyone to contribute in ways that play to their abilities.

- Encourage Diverse Perspectives: Embrace the diversity of thought, background, and experience within the team. Encourage team members to share their unique perspectives, as this diversity can lead to more creative and innovative solutions.

- Rotate Roles and Responsibilities: To keep collaboration dynamic and prevent silos, consider rotating roles and responsibilities within the team. This practice allows team members to develop new skills, gain a broader understanding of the team's work, and build stronger connections with one another.

- Provide Opportunities for Growth: Support the professional and personal development of your team members by providing opportunities for learning and growth. This could include training programs, mentorship, or cross-functional projects. When team members feel that their growth is supported, they are more likely to engage fully in the team's work.

5. Establish Clear Roles and Responsibilities

While collaboration is essential, it's also important for team members to have a clear understanding of their individual roles and responsibilities. Clarity in roles helps prevent confusion, overlap, and inefficiency.

Techniques for Establishing Roles and Responsibilities:

- Define Roles Clearly: Clearly define the roles and responsibilities of each team member at the outset of the project or initiative. Make sure that everyone understands their specific duties and how their work contributes to the team's goals.

- Create Role Descriptions: Consider creating written role descriptions that outline each team member's responsibilities, expectations, and key deliverables. These descriptions can serve as a reference point throughout the project.

- Clarify Decision-Making Authority: Establish clear guidelines for decision-making within the team. Determine who has the authority to make decisions on various aspects of the project and ensure that this is communicated to all team members.

- Encourage Accountability: Foster a culture of accountability by regularly reviewing progress and holding team members responsible for their commitments. When everyone is accountable for their role, the team operates more efficiently and effectively.

6. Promote Effective Communication

Effective communication is the lifeblood of a collaborative team. It ensures that information flows smoothly, misunderstandings are minimized, and everyone is aligned on goals and priorities.

Techniques for Promoting Effective Communication:

- Use the Right Communication Tools: Choose communication tools that suit the needs of your team. This might include project management software, instant messaging platforms, video conferencing, and email. Ensure that all team members are familiar with these tools and use them consistently.

- Encourage Transparency: Promote transparency by sharing information openly and keeping everyone informed about key decisions, progress, and challenges. Transparency builds trust and ensures that everyone is on the same page.

- Provide Regular Updates: Keep team members updated on the status of the project or initiative. Regular updates help prevent surprises, reduce uncertainty, and keep everyone focused on the team's objectives.

- Facilitate Feedback Loops: Create opportunities for team members to provide feedback on the team's processes, communication, and overall collaboration. Act on this feedback to make improvements and address any issues that arise.

7. Encourage Creativity and Innovation

Collaboration is often at its best when team members feel free to explore new ideas, take risks, and innovate. Encouraging creativity within the team can lead to more innovative solutions and better outcomes.

Techniques for Encouraging Creativity:

- Create a Safe Environment for Ideas: Foster an environment where team members feel safe to share their ideas, even if they are unconventional or outside the norm. Encourage brainstorming sessions where all ideas are welcomed without judgment.

- Reward Innovation: Recognize and reward innovative ideas and solutions that emerge from collaboration. This could be through formal recognition, incentives, or simply acknowledging the contribution in team meetings.

- Provide Time for Creative Thinking: Allow team members time to think creatively and explore new ideas. This could involve setting aside dedicated time for brainstorming or encouraging breaks from routine tasks to stimulate fresh thinking.

- Support Risk-Taking: Encourage team members to take calculated risks in their work. When innovation is valued, and the fear of failure is minimized, team members are more likely to experiment and discover new solutions.

8. Foster Continuous Learning and Improvement

An effective and collaborative team is one that continually learns, grows, and improves. By fostering a culture of continuous learning, you ensure that the team remains adaptable, resilient, and capable of tackling new challenges.

Techniques for Fostering Continuous Learning:

- Encourage Reflection: Create opportunities for the team to reflect on their performance, both individually and collectively. This could involve regular retrospectives, where the team discusses what went well, what could be improved, and what lessons were learned.

- Provide Learning Resources: Offer access to learning resources, such as training programs, workshops, online courses, and industry conferences. Encourage team members to take advantage of these opportunities to develop new skills and knowledge.

- Promote a Growth Mindset: Cultivate a growth mindset within the team, where challenges are seen as opportunities for learning and improvement. Encourage team members to embrace challenges, learn from mistakes, and continuously seek ways to enhance their performance.

- Incorporate Feedback for Improvement: Use feedback from team members, stakeholders, and customers to drive continuous improvement. Act on this feedback to refine processes, enhance collaboration, and achieve better results.

Real-Life Examples of Creating Effective and Collaborative Teams

To illustrate how these techniques can be applied in real-life scenarios, consider the following examples:

1. Agile Development Teams in Tech Companies:

- Agile development teams are a prime example of effective and collaborative teams in action. These teams work in short, iterative cycles called sprints, where they set clear goals, assign roles, and collaborate closely to deliver a product increment. Regular stand-up meetings, retrospectives, and feedback loops are integral to the process, ensuring that the team stays aligned, learns continuously, and adapts quickly to changes. The success of agile teams lies in their ability to leverage individual strengths, communicate openly, and maintain a strong focus on collaboration.

2. Cross-Functional Project Teams in Marketing:

- In a marketing agency, a cross-functional project team was assembled to launch a new product campaign for a client. The team included members from various departments, such as creative, strategy, analytics, and client services. To ensure effective collaboration, the team leader defined clear goals and assigned roles based on each member's expertise. Regular check-ins and brainstorming sessions were held to encourage knowledge sharing and innovation. By fostering a culture of inclusivity and creativity, the team was able to deliver a highly successful campaign that exceeded the client's expectations.

Creating an effective and collaborative team requires a combination of clear goals, trust, communication, and a commitment to leveraging the strengths of each team member. By defining clear objectives, building trust and mutual respect, fostering a culture of collaboration, leveraging diversity, establishing clear roles, promoting effective communication, encouraging creativity, and fostering continuous learning, you can build a team that not only works well together but also achieves outstanding results.

As you apply these techniques, you will find that your team becomes more cohesive, productive, and innovative. Collaboration will become second nature, leading to the kind of synergy that drives success and creates lasting value for your organization or group.

Harnessing Diverse Perspectives: Strategies for Integrating Diverse Viewpoints and Ideas

In today's increasingly interconnected world, diversity is not just a value to be upheld—it's a vital source of innovation and competitive advantage. Diverse perspectives bring a wealth of ideas, experiences, and problem-solving approaches that can significantly enhance the outcomes of any team or organization. However, effectively integrating these diverse viewpoints requires intentional strategies to ensure that all voices are heard, valued, and synthesized into cohesive solutions. This chapter explores strategies for harnessing diverse perspectives and integrating them into productive, synergistic outcomes.

Understanding the Value of Diverse Perspectives

Before diving into specific strategies, it's important to understand why diversity of thought is so powerful:

1. Innovation Through Variety:

- Diverse teams are more likely to generate creative solutions because they approach problems from multiple angles. Different cultural backgrounds, educational experiences, and professional expertise contribute to a richer pool of ideas, fostering innovation.

2. Enhanced Problem-Solving:

- When teams draw on a variety of perspectives, they are better equipped to identify potential pitfalls and develop well-rounded solutions. Diverse viewpoints help challenge assumptions, reduce biases, and increase the likelihood of finding effective solutions.

3. Broader Market Understanding:

- A team that reflects a wide range of demographics is better positioned to understand and meet the needs of diverse customer bases. This broader understanding can lead to products, services, and strategies that resonate with a wider audience.

4. Increased Adaptability:

- Teams that embrace diverse perspectives are often more adaptable in the face of change. By being open to different ideas and approaches, these teams can pivot more easily and respond effectively to new challenges and opportunities.

Strategies for Integrating Diverse Viewpoints

1. Foster an Inclusive Culture

Creating an environment where diverse perspectives are valued starts with fostering an inclusive culture. An inclusive culture ensures that all team members feel respected, empowered, and encouraged to contribute their unique viewpoints.

Techniques for Fostering an Inclusive Culture:

- Set the Tone from the Top: Leaders play a critical role in shaping the culture of an organization. By demonstrating a commitment to diversity and inclusion, leaders can set the tone for the rest of the team. This includes making diversity a priority in hiring, promoting diverse voices, and modeling inclusive behavior.

- Create Safe Spaces for Dialogue: Encourage open discussions where team members can share their perspectives without fear of judgment or retribution. This might involve regular team meetings, forums, or informal gatherings where individuals feel comfortable expressing their thoughts and ideas.

- Encourage Allyship: Promote allyship within the team by encouraging members to support and advocate for one another, particularly those from underrepresented groups. Allyship helps create an environment where everyone feels valued and included.

- Celebrate Differences: Recognize and celebrate the diverse backgrounds, experiences, and perspectives within the team. This could involve cultural celebrations, team-building activities that highlight diversity, or simply acknowledging the unique contributions of each team member.

2. Promote Open Communication

Effective integration of diverse perspectives relies on open and transparent communication. When team members communicate openly, they can better understand each other's viewpoints, collaborate effectively, and reach consensus on complex issues.

Techniques for Promoting Open Communication:

- Encourage Active Listening: Active listening is key to understanding diverse perspectives. Train team members to listen attentively, ask clarifying questions, and paraphrase what they've heard to ensure accurate understanding. This practice helps prevent misunderstandings and ensures that all voices are heard.

- Facilitate Structured Discussions: Use structured discussion formats, such as round-robin or fishbowl discussions, to ensure that everyone has an opportunity to speak. These formats help prevent dominant voices from overshadowing others and ensure that all perspectives are considered.

- Practice Transparency: Foster transparency by sharing information openly and ensuring that all team members have access to the same data and insights. Transparency helps level the playing field and allows everyone to contribute equally to decision-making processes.

- Address Communication Barriers: Be mindful of potential communication barriers, such as language differences, cultural nuances, or varying communication styles. Provide resources, such as language support or communication training, to help overcome these barriers and facilitate effective dialogue.

3. Leverage Cross-Functional Teams

Cross-functional teams bring together individuals from different departments, disciplines, or areas of expertise. This diversity within the team enhances creativity, problem-solving, and innovation by integrating a wide range of perspectives.

Techniques for Leveraging Cross-Functional Teams:

- Diversify Team Composition: When forming teams, intentionally include members with diverse skills, experiences, and backgrounds. This diversity ensures that the team can approach problems from multiple angles and generate more innovative solutions.

- Encourage Cross-Pollination of Ideas: Create opportunities for team members to share their knowledge and expertise with others. This might involve cross-training, joint projects, or interdisciplinary workshops that encourage collaboration across different fields.

- Rotate Roles and Responsibilities: Consider rotating team members between different roles or departments to expose them to new perspectives and ideas. This rotation can lead to fresh insights and foster a more holistic understanding of the organization's challenges and opportunities.

- Facilitate Interdepartmental Communication: Encourage regular communication between different departments or teams. This could involve joint meetings, collaborative platforms, or informal networking opportunities that promote the exchange of ideas and foster stronger connections.

4. Implement Collaborative Decision-Making Processes

Collaborative decision-making processes ensure that diverse perspectives are integrated into the final decision. By involving multiple stakeholders in the decision-making process, teams can arrive at more informed and well-rounded outcomes.

Techniques for Collaborative Decision-Making:

- Use Consensus-Building Techniques: Techniques such as brainstorming, nominal group technique, or the Delphi method can help teams build consensus around complex decisions. These methods allow for the integration of diverse viewpoints while ensuring that everyone has a voice in the process.

- Involve All Stakeholders: When making decisions, involve all relevant stakeholders, including those from different departments, levels of the organization, or external partners. This broad involvement ensures that the decision reflects a wide range of perspectives and considerations.

- Encourage Debate and Dialogue: Create an environment where healthy debate and dialogue are encouraged. Diverse perspectives often lead to differing opinions, but through constructive debate, teams can explore all angles of an issue and arrive at the best possible solution.

- Use Decision-Making Tools: Implement decision-making tools, such as decision matrices or SWOT analyses, to help structure the decision-making process. These tools provide a systematic way to evaluate options and integrate diverse perspectives into the final decision.

5. Provide Training and Development Opportunities

Continuous learning and development are crucial for helping team members embrace diversity and effectively integrate diverse perspectives into their work. Training programs can equip individuals with the skills and knowledge needed to collaborate across differences.

Techniques for Training and Development:

- Diversity and Inclusion Training: Offer training programs that focus on diversity, equity, and inclusion. These programs can help team members understand the value of diversity, recognize unconscious biases, and develop strategies for working effectively with diverse groups.

- Cultural Competency Training: Provide cultural competency training to help team members navigate cultural differences and communicate more effectively across cultural boundaries. This training can be particularly valuable in global teams or organizations with diverse workforces.

- Leadership Development Programs: Equip leaders with the skills needed to manage and integrate diverse teams. Leadership development programs should focus on inclusive leadership, emotional intelligence, and effective communication strategies.

- Mentorship and Coaching: Establish mentorship and coaching programs that pair team members with mentors or coaches from different backgrounds or departments. These relationships can provide valuable insights, broaden perspectives, and support professional growth.

6. Foster a Growth Mindset

A growth mindset encourages team members to view challenges as opportunities for learning and growth. This mindset is essential for integrating diverse perspectives, as it promotes openness to new ideas and a willingness to adapt.

Techniques for Fostering a Growth Mindset:

- Encourage Curiosity: Promote a culture of curiosity by encouraging team members to ask questions, seek out new information, and explore different perspectives. Curiosity drives innovation and helps teams stay open to new ideas.

- Celebrate Learning from Mistakes: Create an environment where mistakes are seen as learning opportunities rather than failures. When team members feel safe to take risks and learn from their experiences, they are more likely to embrace diverse perspectives.

- Provide Opportunities for Experimentation: Encourage experimentation and exploration by providing opportunities for team members to test new ideas, pilot projects, or explore alternative approaches. A willingness to experiment fosters creativity and innovation.

- Recognize Effort and Improvement: Acknowledge and reward effort, improvement, and the willingness to learn. Recognizing these qualities reinforces the value of a growth mindset and encourages continued development.

7. Create Collaborative Physical and Virtual Spaces

The physical and virtual environments where teams work can significantly impact their ability to collaborate and integrate diverse perspectives. Thoughtfully designed spaces can enhance communication, creativity, and teamwork.

Techniques for Creating Collaborative Spaces:

- Design Collaborative Workspaces: If possible, design physical workspaces that encourage collaboration. This might include open-plan offices, shared workstations, or breakout areas where team members can gather to discuss ideas informally.

- Leverage Technology for Virtual Collaboration: For remote or hybrid teams, invest in technology that facilitates virtual collaboration. This might include video conferencing tools, collaborative platforms like Slack or Microsoft Teams, and cloud-based document sharing. Ensure that all team members have access to these tools and are trained in their use.

- Create Idea-Sharing Platforms: Establish platforms or forums where team members can share ideas, ask for feedback, and collaborate on projects. These platforms can be virtual (such as an online collaboration tool) or physical (such as a brainstorming wall in the office).

- Encourage Informal Interactions: Create opportunities for informal interactions, both in-person and online. Informal interactions, such as coffee breaks, virtual hangouts, or team lunches, can strengthen relationships and encourage the exchange of diverse perspectives.

Real-Life Examples of Integrating Diverse Perspectives

To illustrate how these strategies can be applied in real-life scenarios, consider the following examples:

1. Tech Company Innovation Labs:

- Many tech companies, such as Google and IBM, have established innovation labs where cross-functional teams work together to develop new products and solutions. These labs bring together engineers, designers, marketers, and customer service representatives from diverse backgrounds. By fostering a culture of open communication, leveraging diverse skills, and promoting experimentation, these labs have produced groundbreaking innovations that drive the company's success.

2. Global Advertising Agency Campaign Development:

- A global advertising agency was tasked with developing a campaign for a multinational client. The agency assembled a cross-functional team with members from different regions, including North America, Europe, and Asia. To integrate diverse perspectives, the team held virtual brainstorming sessions, encouraged open dialogue, and used collaborative decision-making processes. The result was a culturally sensitive and highly effective campaign that resonated with audiences worldwide.

Harnessing diverse perspectives is a powerful strategy for enhancing creativity, problem-solving, and innovation within teams and organizations. By fostering an inclusive culture, promoting open communication, leveraging cross-functional teams, implementing collaborative decision-making processes, providing training and development opportunities, fostering a growth mindset, and creating collaborative physical and virtual spaces, you can effectively integrate diverse viewpoints and ideas into your work.

As you apply these strategies, you will find that your team becomes more dynamic, adaptable, and capable of achieving outstanding results. The ability to harness and integrate diverse perspectives is not only a key driver of success but also a critical factor in building resilient, forward-thinking teams that are prepared to navigate the complexities of today's world.

In the next chapter, we will explore the principles of continuous improvement and how adopting a mindset of lifelong learning can lead to ongoing growth and success in all areas of life.

CHAPTER 07

SHARPEN THE SAW

Continuous Improvement: The Importance of Self-Renewal and Growth

In our fast-paced, ever-evolving world, the importance of continuous improvement and self-renewal cannot be overstated. The concept of "Sharpen the Saw," popularized by Stephen R. Covey, serves as a powerful reminder that taking time to renew and grow is essential for maintaining peak performance and long-term success. This chapter explores the critical importance of self-renewal and growth, emphasizing how they contribute to overall well-being, effectiveness, and sustained achievement.

Understanding the Concept of Self-Renewal

Self-renewal refers to the ongoing process of refreshing and revitalizing yourself physically, mentally,

200

emotionally, and spiritually. It involves taking deliberate actions to maintain and enhance your personal well-being, ensuring that you have the energy, focus, and resilience needed to meet life's challenges and opportunities.

The Four Dimensions of Self-Renewal

1. Physical Renewal:

- Focus on Health and Wellness: Physical renewal involves taking care of your body through proper nutrition, regular exercise, adequate sleep, and stress management. By maintaining physical health, you ensure that you have the energy and vitality needed to perform at your best.

- Importance of Rest and Recovery: Just as tools need to be sharpened to remain effective, your body requires rest and recovery to function optimally. Incorporating regular breaks, vacations, and downtime into your routine is essential for preventing burnout and maintaining long-term productivity.

2. Mental Renewal:

- Commit to Lifelong Learning: Mental renewal involves continuous learning and intellectual growth. Whether through formal education, reading, or exploring new hobbies, challenging your mind keeps it sharp and adaptable.

- Engage in Creative Activities: Engaging in creative activities, such as writing, painting, or problem-solving, stimulates mental growth and encourages innovative thinking. These activities also provide an outlet for self-expression and intellectual exploration.

3. Emotional Renewal:

- Cultivate Healthy Relationships: Emotional renewal is closely tied to the quality of your relationships. Building and maintaining positive, supportive relationships with family, friends, and colleagues provides emotional nourishment and resilience.

- Practice Emotional Intelligence: Developing emotional intelligence—understanding and managing your emotions and those of others—enhances your ability to navigate life's challenges. Practices such as mindfulness, meditation, and self-reflection contribute to emotional balance and well-being.

4. Spiritual Renewal:

- Connect with Your Core Values: Spiritual renewal involves connecting with your core values, beliefs, and purpose. This dimension of self-renewal provides a sense of direction and meaning in life, guiding your decisions and actions.

- Engage in Practices that Inspire You: Whether through meditation, prayer, time in nature, or artistic pursuits, spiritual renewal involves activities that inspire and uplift you.

These practices help you maintain a sense of inner peace and fulfillment, even amidst life's challenges.

The Importance of Continuous Improvement

Continuous improvement is the ongoing process of seeking ways to enhance your skills, knowledge, and effectiveness. It is rooted in the belief that there is always room for growth and that incremental changes can lead to significant long-term gains.

Benefits of Continuous Improvement

1. Sustained Personal and Professional Growth:

- Continuous improvement ensures that you are constantly developing and refining your skills and knowledge. This ongoing growth keeps you competitive in your career and allows you to achieve personal milestones that contribute to a fulfilling life.

2. Adaptability and Resilience:

- In a rapidly changing world, the ability to adapt is crucial. Continuous improvement fosters adaptability by encouraging you to embrace change, learn new skills, and remain open to new opportunities. This adaptability, in turn, builds resilience, helping you navigate challenges and bounce back from setbacks.

3. Increased Self-Confidence:

- As you make progress and achieve your goals through continuous improvement, your self-confidence grows. This increased confidence empowers you to take on new challenges, pursue ambitious goals, and approach life with a positive, proactive mindset.

4. Enhanced Problem-Solving Abilities:

- Continuous improvement sharpens your problem-solving abilities by encouraging critical thinking, creativity, and innovation. As you refine your skills and expand your knowledge, you become better equipped to tackle complex challenges and find effective solutions.

5. Greater Life Satisfaction:

- The pursuit of continuous improvement leads to a greater sense of accomplishment and satisfaction. By consistently striving to become the best version of yourself, you create a life that is rich in purpose, fulfillment, and joy.

Strategies for Self-Renewal and Growth

1. Set Clear and Achievable Goals:

- Define Your Objectives: Start by setting clear, specific goals for your personal and professional growth. These goals should be aligned with your values and long-term vision, providing a roadmap for your continuous improvement journey.

- Break Goals into Manageable Steps: Large goals can be overwhelming, so break them down into smaller, actionable steps. This approach makes it easier to track your progress and maintain momentum.

2. Commit to Lifelong Learning:

- Engage in Ongoing Education: Whether through formal courses, workshops, or self-directed learning, commit to expanding your knowledge and skills regularly. Stay curious and seek out new learning opportunities that align with your interests and goals.

- Explore New Hobbies and Interests: Exploring new hobbies and interests stimulates mental growth and creativity. Whether it's learning a new language, picking up a musical instrument, or trying out a new sport, these activities keep your mind engaged and open to new experiences.

3. Prioritize Health and Wellness:

- Adopt a Balanced Lifestyle: Ensure that your lifestyle supports physical, mental, emotional, and spiritual well-being. This might involve adopting a balanced diet, exercising regularly, getting enough sleep, and managing stress effectively.

- Incorporate Regular Breaks and Downtime: Avoid burnout by incorporating regular breaks, vacations, and downtime into your routine. This time away from work and daily responsibilities is essential for physical and mental rejuvenation.

4. Cultivate Emotional Intelligence:

- Practice Self-Awareness: Develop self-awareness by regularly reflecting on your thoughts, emotions, and behaviors. Understanding your emotional triggers and responses helps you manage them more effectively.

- Strengthen Relationships: Build and maintain strong, supportive relationships with others. Practice empathy, active listening, and effective communication to enhance your emotional connections and contribute to emotional renewal.

5. Engage in Spiritual Practices:

- Connect with Your Inner Self: Regularly engage in activities that connect you with your inner self and core values. This might involve meditation, prayer, journaling, or spending time in nature.

- Seek Inspiration and Purpose: Pursue activities that inspire and uplift you, whether it's through artistic expression, volunteer work, or spiritual study. These practices help you maintain a sense of purpose and fulfillment.

6. Embrace a Growth Mindset:

- View Challenges as Opportunities: Cultivate a growth mindset by viewing challenges and setbacks as opportunities for learning and growth. Embrace the idea that your abilities and intelligence can be developed through effort and perseverance.

- Celebrate Progress: Recognize and celebrate your progress, no matter how small. Acknowledge the effort you've put into your growth and use it as motivation to continue improving.

7. Seek Feedback and Reflection:

- Invite Constructive Feedback: Regularly seek feedback from others on your performance and progress. Constructive feedback provides valuable insights into areas where you can improve and grow.

- Reflect on Your Journey: Take time to reflect on your continuous improvement journey. Consider what you've learned, how you've grown, and what adjustments you can make to stay on track.

Real-Life Examples of Self-Renewal and Continuous Improvement

To illustrate the importance of self-renewal and continuous improvement, consider the following examples:

1. Professional Development:

- Example: Sarah, a marketing professional, realized that the digital marketing landscape was evolving rapidly. To stay competitive, she committed to continuous learning by enrolling in online courses, attending industry conferences, and participating in professional networks. Over time, Sarah's efforts paid off as she developed new skills, advanced in her career, and became a sought-after expert in her field.

2. Personal Growth:

- Example: John, a father of two, found that the demands of work and family were leaving him physically and emotionally drained. Recognizing the need for self-renewal, John made changes to his lifestyle, including regular exercise, meditation, and setting aside time for hobbies he enjoyed. These changes not only improved John's health and well-being but also enhanced his ability to be present and engaged with his family.

Self-renewal and continuous improvement are essential for achieving long-term success, well-being, and fulfillment. By committing to ongoing growth and taking deliberate actions to renew yourself physically, mentally, emotionally, and spiritually, you ensure that you remain resilient, adaptable, and capable of reaching your full potential.

The strategies outlined in this chapter—setting clear goals, committing to lifelong learning, prioritizing health and wellness, cultivating emotional intelligence, engaging in spiritual practices, embracing a growth mindset, and seeking feedback and reflection—provide a roadmap for your journey of self-renewal and continuous improvement.

As you apply these strategies, you will find that you are better equipped to meet life's challenges, seize opportunities, and create a life that is rich in purpose, achievement, and joy. The process of sharpening the saw is ongoing, but the rewards are well worth the effort, leading to a life of sustained growth, balance, and fulfillment.

In the final chapter, we will explore how to bring all these habits together, creating a balanced and harmonious life that allows you to achieve your goals while maintaining well-being and fulfillment.

Sharpen the Saw

Techniques for Maintaining Physical, Mental, Emotional, and Spiritual Well-Being

Maintaining well-being across all dimensions—physical, mental, emotional, and spiritual—is essential for leading a balanced, fulfilling life. When these areas are nurtured and in harmony, you're better equipped to handle life's challenges, achieve your goals, and enjoy a sense of peace and contentment. This chapter explores practical techniques for maintaining well-being in each of these dimensions, providing you with a comprehensive approach to self-care and personal growth.

1. Physical Well-Being

Physical well-being is the foundation of your overall health. It involves taking care of your body through proper nutrition, regular exercise, adequate sleep, and effective stress management. By prioritizing your physical health, you ensure that you have the energy and stamina needed to pursue your goals and enjoy life to the fullest.

Techniques for Maintaining Physical Well-Being:

- Adopt a Balanced Diet:

- Focus on Nutrient-Rich Foods: A balanced diet is rich in fruits, vegetables, whole grains, lean proteins, and healthy fats. These foods provide the essential nutrients your body needs to function optimally.

- Practice Portion Control: Pay attention to portion sizes to avoid overeating. Eating mindfully, without distractions, can help you better regulate your food intake.

- Stay Hydrated: Drink plenty of water throughout the day to stay hydrated. Water is essential for maintaining energy levels, supporting digestion, and promoting overall health.

- Engage in Regular Exercise:

- Incorporate Aerobic Exercise: Aim for at least 150 minutes of moderate-intensity aerobic exercise, such as walking, cycling, or swimming, each week. Aerobic exercise strengthens your heart and lungs, boosts your mood, and helps manage weight.

- Include Strength Training: Engage in strength training exercises, such as weightlifting or bodyweight exercises, at least two days a week. Strength training builds muscle, supports bone health, and improves overall physical function.

- Prioritize Flexibility and Balance: Incorporate activities that enhance flexibility and balance, such as yoga or stretching exercises. These activities help prevent injuries and improve mobility.

- Ensure Adequate Sleep:

- Establish a Consistent Sleep Routine: Go to bed and wake up at the same time each day, even on weekends. A consistent sleep schedule helps regulate your body's internal clock and improves sleep quality.

- Create a Relaxing Bedtime Routine: Engage in calming activities, such as reading, taking a warm bath, or practicing relaxation techniques, before bed. A bedtime routine signals to your body that it's time to wind down.

- Optimize Your Sleep Environment: Ensure that your sleep environment is conducive to rest by keeping your bedroom cool, dark, and quiet. Invest in a comfortable mattress and pillows that support restful sleep.

- Manage Stress Effectively:

- Practice Relaxation Techniques: Techniques such as deep breathing, progressive muscle relaxation, and guided imagery can help reduce stress and promote relaxation.

- Engage in Physical Activity: Exercise is a powerful stress reliever. Regular physical activity helps lower stress hormones, release endorphins, and improve mood.

- Prioritize Self-Care: Make time for activities that you enjoy and that help you relax, such as spending time in nature, pursuing hobbies, or practicing mindfulness.

2. Mental Well-Being

Mental well-being involves maintaining cognitive health and stimulating your mind through continuous learning, creative expression, and problem-solving. A healthy mind is sharp, adaptable, and resilient, allowing you to navigate life's challenges with clarity and confidence.

Techniques for Maintaining Mental Well-Being:

- Engage in Lifelong Learning:

- Pursue Educational Opportunities: Take advantage of formal education opportunities, such as courses, workshops, or certifications, to expand your knowledge and skills.

- Read Regularly: Reading books, articles, and research papers on a variety of topics stimulates your mind and keeps you informed. Make reading a daily habit to continuously feed your intellect.

- Explore New Hobbies: Trying out new hobbies, such as learning a musical instrument, taking up a craft, or mastering a new language, keeps your brain engaged and challenges your cognitive abilities.

- Practice Critical Thinking:

- Analyze and Evaluate Information: Develop your critical thinking skills by analyzing and evaluating the information you encounter. Question assumptions, consider alternative viewpoints, and weigh evidence before forming conclusions.

- Engage in Intellectual Discussions: Participate in discussions and debates on topics of interest. Engaging with others in meaningful conversations helps refine your thinking and exposes you to diverse perspectives.

- Solve Puzzles and Games: Activities such as crossword puzzles, Sudoku, chess, and strategy games challenge your mind and improve problem-solving abilities.

- Foster Creativity:

- Engage in Creative Expression: Whether it's writing, painting, music, or other forms of artistic expression, creativity stimulates your mind and allows you to explore new ideas.

- Brainstorm New Ideas: Regularly set aside time for brainstorming sessions where you generate new ideas or solutions to challenges. Encourage free thinking without judgment during these sessions.

- Experiment with New Approaches: Challenge yourself to try new approaches in your work or personal projects. Experimenting with different methods fosters creativity and innovation.

- Practice Mindfulness and Meditation:

- Cultivate Present-Moment Awareness: Mindfulness involves focusing on the present moment without judgment. Practice mindfulness techniques to improve concentration, reduce mental clutter, and enhance clarity.

- Incorporate Meditation into Your Routine: Regular meditation practice helps calm the mind, reduce stress, and improve mental focus. Start with just a few minutes a day and gradually increase the duration as you become more comfortable.

3. Emotional Well-Being

Emotional well-being involves understanding, managing, and expressing your emotions in a healthy and constructive manner. It also includes building and maintaining strong relationships, developing emotional intelligence, and practicing self-compassion.

Techniques for Maintaining Emotional Well-Being:

- Develop Emotional Intelligence:

- Enhance Self-Awareness: Regularly reflect on your emotions, thoughts, and behaviors. Recognize your emotional triggers and patterns, and understand how they influence your actions and interactions.

- Practice Empathy: Put yourself in others' shoes to understand their emotions and perspectives. Empathy strengthens relationships and enhances your ability to connect with others on an emotional level.

- Improve Emotional Regulation: Learn techniques for managing your emotions, such as deep breathing, journaling, or talking with a trusted friend. These practices help you respond to emotions in a constructive way rather than reacting impulsively.

- Build and Maintain Healthy Relationships:

- Prioritize Quality Time: Spend meaningful time with loved ones, engaging in activities that foster connection and bonding. Whether it's family dinners, outings with friends, or quiet moments with a partner, prioritize time with those who matter most.

- Communicate Openly and Honestly: Practice open and honest communication with the people in your life. Share your thoughts and feelings, listen actively to others, and address conflicts with compassion and understanding.

- Set Boundaries: Establish and maintain healthy boundaries in your relationships to protect your emotional well-being. Boundaries help prevent burnout and ensure that your relationships remain respectful and mutually supportive.

- Practice Self-Compassion:

- Be Kind to Yourself: Treat yourself with the same kindness and understanding that you would offer to a friend. Acknowledge your strengths and achievements, and be gentle with yourself when you encounter setbacks.

- Challenge Negative Self-Talk: When you catch yourself engaging in negative self-talk, challenge these thoughts by reframing them in a more positive and realistic light. Replace self-criticism with self-encouragement.

- Practice Gratitude: Regularly practice gratitude by reflecting on the positive aspects of your life. Keeping a gratitude journal or simply taking a few moments each day to acknowledge what you're thankful for can enhance your emotional well-being.

- Engage in Stress-Relieving Activities:

- Pursue Relaxation Techniques: Engage in activities that promote relaxation, such as deep breathing exercises, yoga, or spending time in nature. These practices help reduce stress and improve emotional resilience.

- Express Your Emotions Creatively: Creative outlets, such as writing, drawing, or music, provide a way to express and process your emotions. Use these activities to explore and release feelings in a healthy manner.

    - Seek Support When Needed: Don't hesitate to seek support from friends, family, or a mental health professional when you're struggling with emotional challenges. Talking about your feelings and receiving guidance can be incredibly healing.

4. Spiritual Well-Being

Spiritual well-being involves connecting with your inner self, core values, and sense of purpose. It includes engaging in practices that inspire and uplift you, fostering a sense of peace, fulfillment, and connection with something greater than yourself.

Techniques for Maintaining Spiritual Well-Being:

- Connect with Your Core Values:

    - Reflect on Your Beliefs: Regularly reflect on your core values and beliefs, considering how they guide your decisions and actions. Understanding what matters most to you provides a sense of direction and purpose in life.

    - Align Your Actions with Your Values: Strive to live in alignment with your values, making choices that reflect your true self. This alignment fosters authenticity and a deep sense of fulfillment.

    - Engage in Spiritual Practices:

- Practice Meditation or Prayer: Regular meditation or prayer helps you connect with your inner self and cultivate a sense of inner peace. These practices provide an opportunity for introspection and spiritual growth.

- Spend Time in Nature: Nature has a profound ability to restore and rejuvenate the spirit. Spend time in natural settings, whether it's a walk in the park, a hike in the mountains, or simply sitting by a body of water, to reconnect with the beauty and tranquility of the natural world.

- Explore Spiritual Teachings: Delve into spiritual teachings, whether through reading, attending religious or spiritual gatherings, or participating in study groups. Exploring different philosophies and traditions can deepen your understanding of life's meaning and purpose.

- Seek Inspiration and Purpose:

- Engage in Purposeful Activities: Engage in activities that give you a sense of purpose, whether it's through volunteering, mentoring, or pursuing a passion project. Purposeful activities provide a sense of fulfillment and contribute to your overall well-being.

- Surround Yourself with Inspirational Influences: Surround yourself with people, books, music, and art that inspire and uplift you. These influences can provide motivation, guidance, and a renewed sense of purpose.

- Practice Gratitude and Mindfulness:

- Cultivate a Gratitude Practice: Regularly practice gratitude by reflecting on the blessings in your life. Acknowledging what you're thankful for helps shift your focus to the positive aspects of life and fosters a sense of contentment.

- Live Mindfully: Practice mindfulness by being fully present in each moment. Whether you're eating, walking, or engaging in a conversation, mindfulness enhances your spiritual connection and deepens your appreciation for life's simple pleasures.

Real-Life Examples of Maintaining Well-Being

To illustrate how these techniques can be applied in real-life scenarios, consider the following examples:

1. Work-Life Balance:

- Example: Emily, a corporate executive, found that her demanding job was taking a toll on her physical and emotional well-being. To restore balance, she committed to a daily exercise routine, adopted a balanced diet, and made time for meditation each morning. Emily also prioritized spending quality time with her family and set boundaries to prevent work from encroaching on her personal life. These changes not only improved her well-being but also enhanced her performance at work.

2. Creative Renewal:

- Example: David, an artist, was feeling creatively blocked and mentally exhausted. Recognizing the need for mental and spiritual renewal, he decided to take a sabbatical to travel and explore new cultures. During his travels, David engaged in creative activities, such as photography and journaling, and spent time in nature to reconnect with his inner self. This period of renewal reignited David's creativity and provided fresh inspiration for his art.

Maintaining well-being across all dimensions—physical, mental, emotional, and spiritual—is essential for leading a balanced and fulfilling life. By prioritizing self-care and adopting practices that nurture each of these dimensions, you ensure that you remain resilient, adaptable, and capable of achieving your goals.

The techniques outlined in this chapter—adopting a balanced diet, engaging in regular exercise, committing to lifelong learning, practicing emotional intelligence, engaging in spiritual practices, and embracing a growth mindset—provide a comprehensive approach to maintaining well-being. As you integrate these practices into your daily life, you will find that you are better equipped to handle life's challenges, enjoy deeper connections with others, and experience a greater sense of peace and fulfillment.

Creating a Balanced Life: Strategies for Regular Self-Assessment and Personal Development

In the pursuit of a fulfilling and successful life, balance is key. Creating a balanced life involves regularly assessing your personal and professional development, setting priorities, and making intentional choices that align with your values and goals. It's about ensuring that the different aspects of your life—work, relationships, health, personal growth—are in harmony, allowing you to thrive in all areas. This chapter explores strategies for regular self-assessment and personal development, providing you with the tools to create and maintain a balanced life.

Understanding the Importance of a Balanced Life

A balanced life is not about distributing equal time to every aspect of your life but about giving appropriate attention to what matters most to you. It involves recognizing when one area of your life is out of sync and making the necessary adjustments to restore equilibrium. Living a balanced life leads to greater well-being, productivity, and overall satisfaction.

Benefits of a Balanced Life

1. Improved Well-Being:

- Balance in life contributes to physical, mental, emotional, and spiritual well-being. When you pay attention to all aspects of your life, you reduce stress, prevent burnout, and enhance your overall health.

2. Greater Productivity:

- A balanced life allows you to focus more effectively on your tasks and responsibilities. By managing your time and energy wisely, you can achieve more without sacrificing your well-being.

3. Enhanced Relationships:

- Prioritizing balance helps you maintain strong and meaningful relationships. When you dedicate time to nurturing your connections with family, friends, and colleagues, you build deeper bonds and create a support system.

4. Increased Personal Fulfillment:

- Living in balance ensures that you are not neglecting your passions, interests, or personal growth. This leads to a more fulfilling life, where you can pursue your goals and dreams while maintaining harmony in other areas.

Strategies for Regular Self-Assessment

Self-assessment is a crucial tool for maintaining balance in your life. It involves regularly evaluating where you are in relation to your goals, values, and priorities, and making adjustments as needed. Through self-assessment, you gain insights into what is working well and what needs improvement.

Techniques for Effective Self-Assessment:

1. Set Aside Time for Reflection:

- Schedule Regular Check-Ins: Make it a habit to set aside time for self-reflection, whether it's daily, weekly, or monthly. During these check-ins, review your goals, assess your progress, and consider how balanced you feel in different areas of your life.

- Create a Quiet Space for Reflection: Choose a quiet, comfortable place where you can reflect without distractions. This space allows you to think clearly and deeply about your life's direction and balance.

2. Use Self-Assessment Tools:

- Life Balance Wheel: The Life Balance Wheel is a visual tool that helps you assess different areas of your life, such as work, health, relationships, and personal growth. By rating your satisfaction in each area, you can identify where you may need to focus more attention.

- Journaling: Keeping a journal is an effective way to track your thoughts, feelings, and progress over time. Use your journal to reflect on your achievements, challenges, and areas where you want to improve balance.

- SWOT Analysis: Conduct a personal SWOT analysis (Strengths, Weaknesses, Opportunities, Threats) to assess your current situation and identify areas for growth. This analysis helps you understand where you excel, where you need to develop, and how external factors may impact your balance.

3. Evaluate Your Priorities:

- Identify Your Core Values: Reflect on your core values and how they influence your decisions and actions. Ensure that your life choices align with these values, as this alignment is key to achieving balance.

- Assess Your Time Allocation: Take a close look at how you spend your time each day. Are you dedicating enough time to the things that matter most to you? If not, consider how you can adjust your schedule to better reflect your priorities.

- Consider Long-Term Goals: Evaluate your long-term goals and how your current actions are contributing to or detracting from them. Make sure that your daily activities are moving you closer to your desired outcomes.

4. Seek Feedback from Others:

- Ask Trusted Individuals: Sometimes, others can offer valuable insights that you may not see yourself. Seek feedback from trusted friends, family members, or colleagues about how they perceive your life balance and where they think you could improve.

- Participate in Group Discussions: Engage in discussions with peers or mentors who share similar goals. Group discussions can provide different perspectives and help you see areas for growth that you may have overlooked.

5. Set New Goals and Adjustments:

- Review and Revise Goals: Based on your self-assessment, review and revise your goals to ensure they are still relevant and achievable. If your circumstances or priorities have changed, adjust your goals accordingly.

- Create an Action Plan: Develop a clear action plan to address areas where you need more balance. Break down your plan into specific, actionable steps that you can implement gradually over time.

- Monitor Your Progress: Regularly monitor your progress toward achieving a more balanced life. Celebrate your successes and make adjustments as needed to stay on track.

Strategies for Personal Development

Personal development is an ongoing process that involves setting goals, acquiring new skills, and continuously improving yourself. By prioritizing personal development, you not only enhance your abilities but also contribute to a more balanced and fulfilling life.

Techniques for Effective Personal Development:

1. Set SMART Goals:

- Specific: Define clear and specific goals that outline exactly what you want to achieve. For example, instead of saying, "I want to be healthier," set a specific goal such as, "I want to lose 10 pounds in three months by exercising three times a week and eating a balanced diet."

- Measurable: Ensure that your goals are measurable so that you can track your progress. For example, if your goal is to read more, set a measurable target, such as reading one book per month.

- Achievable: Set goals that are challenging but achievable. Consider your current circumstances, resources, and time constraints when setting your goals.

- Relevant: Ensure that your goals are relevant to your values and long-term objectives. Focus on goals that will have a meaningful impact on your life.

- Time-Bound: Set deadlines for achieving your goals. Having a timeframe creates a sense of urgency and helps you stay focused.

2. Commit to Lifelong Learning:

- Engage in Continuous Education: Make learning a lifelong habit by seeking out opportunities to expand your knowledge and skills. This could involve taking courses, attending workshops, or simply reading books on topics that interest you.

- Explore New Areas of Interest: Don't be afraid to step outside your comfort zone and explore new areas of interest. Whether it's learning a new language, trying a new hobby, or pursuing a different career path, expanding your horizons contributes to personal growth.

- Stay Curious: Cultivate a mindset of curiosity and openness to new ideas. Ask questions, seek out new experiences, and remain open to different perspectives.

3. Build and Maintain Healthy Habits:

- Identify Key Habits: Identify the habits that contribute most to your well-being and success, such as regular exercise, healthy eating, or time management. Focus on building and maintaining these habits consistently.

- Use Habit-Tracking Tools: Habit-tracking tools, such as apps or journals, can help you monitor your progress and stay accountable. Track your habits daily or weekly to ensure you're staying on course.

- Reward Yourself: Celebrate your achievements and reward yourself for maintaining positive habits. Rewards can be as simple as taking a day off to relax or treating yourself to something you enjoy.

4. Develop Emotional Intelligence:

- Enhance Self-Awareness: Regularly reflect on your emotions, thoughts, and behaviors. Understand how your emotions influence your actions and decisions, and work on managing them effectively.

- Strengthen Interpersonal Skills: Practice empathy, active listening, and effective communication to build stronger relationships with others. Emotional intelligence is key to navigating social interactions and maintaining balance in your personal and professional life.

- Manage Stress and Emotions: Develop techniques for managing stress and emotions, such as mindfulness, meditation, or deep breathing exercises. Emotional resilience is essential for maintaining balance in challenging situations.

5. Create a Supportive Environment:

- Surround Yourself with Positive Influences: Surround yourself with people who support your goals and encourage your personal growth. Positive relationships provide motivation, guidance, and accountability.

- Organize Your Space: Create an environment that supports your personal development goals. Whether it's a clutter-free workspace, a home gym, or a reading nook, your physical environment should reflect your priorities and support your efforts.

- Limit Negative Influences: Identify and minimize influences that detract from your balance and personal growth, such as toxic relationships, distractions, or negative self-talk. Focus on cultivating an environment that nurtures your well-being and success.

6. Practice Gratitude and Mindfulness:

- Cultivate a Gratitude Practice: Regularly practice gratitude by reflecting on the positive aspects of your life. Keeping a gratitude journal or simply taking a few moments each day to acknowledge what you're thankful for can enhance your emotional well-being and help you maintain a positive outlook.

- Live Mindfully: Practice mindfulness by being fully present in each moment. Whether you're eating, walking, or engaging in a conversation, mindfulness enhances your spiritual connection and deepens your appreciation for life's simple pleasures.

7. Seek Balance in All Areas of Life:

- Balance Work and Personal Life: Set boundaries to prevent work from encroaching on your personal life. Prioritize time for family, friends, hobbies, and self-care to ensure that all aspects of your life are in harmony.

- Practice Self-Compassion: Treat yourself with the same kindness and understanding that you would offer to a friend. Acknowledge your strengths and achievements, and be gentle with yourself when you encounter setbacks.

- Align Actions with Values: Ensure that your daily actions align with your core values. This alignment fosters authenticity and a deep sense of fulfillment.

Real-Life Examples of Balancing Life Through Self-Assessment and Personal Development

To illustrate how these strategies can be applied in real-life scenarios, consider the following examples:

1. Balancing Career and Family:

- Example: Laura, a successful entrepreneur, found herself struggling to balance her growing business with her responsibilities as a mother. Through regular self-assessment, she realized that she was neglecting her personal life in favor of work. Laura decided to set clearer boundaries by scheduling dedicated family time and delegating more tasks at work. She also committed to personal development by taking courses in time management and emotional intelligence. These changes allowed Laura to achieve a better balance between her career and family life, leading to greater fulfillment and well-being.

2. Prioritizing Health and Personal Growth:

- Example: James, a software developer, noticed that his sedentary lifestyle was affecting his health and productivity. Through self-assessment, he identified the need to prioritize physical well-being and personal growth. James set specific goals for regular exercise, improved nutrition, and continuous learning. He started attending fitness classes, preparing healthy meals, and enrolling in online courses to expand his skills. By integrating these habits into his daily routine, James not only improved his health but also enhanced his career prospects and overall life satisfaction.

Creating a balanced life requires regular self-assessment and a commitment to personal development. By taking the time to reflect on your priorities, set meaningful goals, and make intentional choices, you can achieve harmony in all areas of your life.

The strategies outlined in this chapter—setting aside time for reflection, using self-assessment tools, evaluating your priorities, seeking feedback, setting new goals, committing to lifelong learning, building healthy habits, developing emotional intelligence, creating a supportive environment, practicing gratitude and mindfulness, and seeking balance in all areas of life—provide a roadmap for achieving and maintaining balance.

As you apply these strategies, you will find that your life becomes more balanced, fulfilling, and aligned with your values and goals. Regular self-assessment and personal development are ongoing processes, but the rewards are well worth the effort, leading to a life of sustained growth, balance, and fulfillment.

CHAPTER 08

CULTIVATE AN ABUNDANCE MENTALITY

The Abundance vs. Scarcity Mentality: Understanding the Difference and Its Impact on Effectiveness

Our mindset shapes the way we perceive the world, influences our decisions, and determines the quality of our lives. Two prevalent mindsets that significantly impact our effectiveness in both personal and professional settings are the abundance mentality and the scarcity mentality. These mindsets affect how we view opportunities, resources, relationships, and our overall sense of well-being. In this chapter, we will explore the fundamental differences between the abundance mentality and the scarcity mentality, and examine how each mindset impacts effectiveness, success, and fulfillment.

Understanding the Abundance Mentality

An abundance mentality is rooted in the belief that there is enough—enough resources, opportunities, success, and love for everyone. This mindset is characterized by a positive outlook on life, a sense of generosity, and a willingness to share and collaborate. People with an abundance mentality see possibilities where others see limitations and approach challenges with confidence and optimism.

Key Characteristics of an Abundance Mentality

1. Optimism and Positivity:

- Individuals with an abundance mentality tend to have a positive outlook on life. They believe that challenges can be overcome, that opportunities are plentiful, and that setbacks are temporary. This optimism drives them to take proactive steps toward their goals and to view difficulties as opportunities for growth.

2. Generosity and Collaboration:

- An abundance mentality fosters a spirit of generosity. People who embrace this mindset are willing to share their knowledge, resources, and success with others. They believe that helping others succeed does not diminish their own achievements but rather contributes to a collective success.

3. Focus on Growth and Possibility:

- Those with an abundance mentality focus on possibilities rather than limitations. They are open to new ideas, willing to take risks, and see failure as a learning opportunity. This growth-oriented mindset encourages continuous improvement and innovation.

4. Trust and Security:

- An abundance mentality is grounded in trust—trust in oneself, in others, and in the process of life. This trust leads to a sense of security, allowing individuals to take calculated risks, build strong relationships, and remain resilient in the face of adversity.

5. Gratitude and Contentment:

- People with an abundance mentality practice gratitude regularly. They appreciate what they have and focus on the positive aspects of their lives. This sense of contentment reduces feelings of envy or competition and promotes a sense of well-being.

The Impact of an Abundance Mentality on Effectiveness

1. Enhanced Creativity and Innovation:

- An abundance mentality encourages creative thinking and innovation. By focusing on possibilities and embracing a growth mindset, individuals are more likely to explore new ideas, experiment with different approaches, and find innovative solutions to problems. This creativity leads to greater effectiveness in achieving goals and overcoming challenges.

2. Stronger Relationships and Collaboration:

- The generosity and collaboration that characterize an abundance mentality lead to stronger relationships, both personally and professionally. When individuals are willing to share their success and support others, they build trust and rapport, fostering a collaborative environment that enhances team effectiveness.

3. Increased Resilience and Adaptability:

- Trust and security, hallmarks of an abundance mentality, contribute to greater resilience and adaptability. Individuals who believe in their ability to overcome challenges are more likely to persevere in the face of setbacks and adapt to changing circumstances. This resilience enhances their effectiveness in navigating complex situations.

4. Greater Life Satisfaction and Fulfillment:

- An abundance mentality promotes a sense of gratitude and contentment, leading to greater life satisfaction and fulfillment. When individuals appreciate what they have and focus on the positive aspects of their lives, they are more likely to experience joy and well-being. This satisfaction fuels their motivation and effectiveness in all areas of life.

Understanding the Scarcity Mentality

In contrast, a scarcity mentality is rooted in the belief that there is a limited amount of resources, opportunities, and success available. This mindset is characterized by fear, competition, and a focus on limitations. People with a scarcity mentality often view life as a zero-sum game, where someone else's gain is perceived as their loss.

Key Characteristics of a Scarcity Mentality

1. Fear and Anxiety:

- Individuals with a scarcity mentality often operate from a place of fear and anxiety. They worry that there isn't enough to go around—whether it's money, time, love, or opportunities. This fear leads to stress and a constant sense of insecurity.

2. Competition and Hoarding:

- A scarcity mentality fosters a competitive mindset, where individuals feel the need to hoard resources, protect their interests, and view others as threats. This competition can lead to unhealthy rivalries, strained relationships, and a reluctance to share knowledge or collaborate.

3. Focus on Limitations:

- People with a scarcity mentality tend to focus on what they lack rather than what they have. This focus on limitations leads to a negative outlook, a reluctance to take risks, and a tendency to shy away from challenges. As a result, they may miss out on opportunities for growth and development.

4. Distrust and Insecurity:

- Distrust is a common trait of the scarcity mentality. Individuals may distrust others, believing that they must protect themselves from being taken advantage of or losing out. This insecurity can lead to isolation, poor decision-making, and an inability to build strong, supportive relationships.

5. Envy and Resentment:

- A scarcity mentality often breeds envy and resentment. Individuals may feel envious of others' success and resentful of their own perceived lack. This negative emotional state can lead to bitterness and a sense of dissatisfaction with life.

The Impact of a Scarcity Mentality on Effectiveness

1. Limited Creativity and Innovation:

- A scarcity mentality stifles creativity and innovation. When individuals focus on limitations and fear failure, they are less likely to take risks or think outside the box. This fear-driven approach limits their ability to find effective solutions to problems and hinders their overall effectiveness.

2. Weakened Relationships and Collaboration:

- The competition and distrust that characterize a scarcity mentality can weaken relationships and hinder collaboration. When individuals are focused on protecting their own interests, they may be less willing to share information, offer support, or work together toward common goals. This lack of collaboration reduces team effectiveness and can lead to conflict.

3. Decreased Resilience and Adaptability:

- A scarcity mentality reduces resilience and adaptability. Individuals who operate from a place of fear and insecurity may struggle to cope with challenges and changes. They may be more likely to give up when faced with obstacles and less able to adapt to new circumstances, reducing their effectiveness in dynamic environments.

4. Lower Life Satisfaction and Fulfillment:

- The envy, resentment, and focus on limitations that come with a scarcity mentality contribute to lower life satisfaction and fulfillment. Individuals may constantly feel dissatisfied with their lives, focusing on what they lack rather than appreciating what they have. This dissatisfaction can lead to a lack of motivation and a reduced sense of purpose, further diminishing their effectiveness.

Shifting from a Scarcity to an Abundance Mentality

The good news is that it is possible to shift from a scarcity mentality to an abundance mentality. By consciously adopting new habits, reframing your thoughts, and cultivating positive behaviors, you can develop an abundance mindset that enhances your effectiveness and overall well-being.

Strategies for Cultivating an Abundance Mentality:

1. Practice Gratitude:

- Keep a Gratitude Journal: Regularly write down the things you are grateful for in a journal. This practice shifts your focus from what you lack to what you have, fostering a sense of abundance and contentment.

- Express Gratitude to Others: Take the time to express gratitude to the people in your life. Whether through a simple thank-you note, a verbal acknowledgment, or a gesture of appreciation, showing gratitude strengthens relationships and reinforces an abundance mindset.

2. Embrace a Growth Mindset:

- View Challenges as Opportunities: Reframe challenges as opportunities for growth and learning. Instead of fearing failure, embrace it as a natural part of the learning process and a stepping stone to success.

- Celebrate Others' Successes: Shift your perspective from competition to collaboration by celebrating the successes of others. Recognize that someone else's success does not diminish your own and that there is enough success to go around.

3. Focus on Possibilities:

- Look for Opportunities in Every Situation: Train yourself to see opportunities where others see limitations. When faced with a problem, ask yourself, "What possibilities does this situation present?" This mindset encourages creative thinking and innovation.

- Surround Yourself with Positive Influences: Surround yourself with people who have an abundance mentality. Positive influences can help reinforce your mindset and encourage you to focus on possibilities rather than limitations.

4. Cultivate Generosity:

- Share Your Knowledge and Resources: Practice generosity by sharing your knowledge, resources, and success with others. Whether through mentoring, volunteering, or simply offering support, generosity fosters a sense of abundance and strengthens relationships.

- Give Without Expecting Anything in Return: Embrace the mindset of giving without expecting anything in return. This approach reinforces the belief that there is enough to go around and that helping others does not diminish your own success.

5. Build Trust and Security:

- Develop Self-Confidence: Work on building your self-confidence and trust in your abilities. When you believe in yourself, you are more likely to take risks, pursue opportunities, and remain resilient in the face of challenges.

- Nurture Supportive Relationships: Build strong, supportive relationships with others. Trusting relationships provide a sense of security and reinforce the abundance mentality by creating a network of mutual support.

Real-Life Examples of the Abundance and Scarcity Mentalities

To illustrate the difference between these mindsets and their impact, consider the following examples:

1. Professional Collaboration:

- Abundance Mentality: Sarah, a marketing manager, believes that collaboration leads to better outcomes for everyone involved. She openly shares her strategies with colleagues, offers to mentor junior team members, and collaborates with other departments on projects. As a result, Sarah's team consistently produces high-quality work, and she is known for her leadership and generosity.

- Scarcity Mentality: Tom, another marketing manager, views his colleagues as competitors. He hoards information, is reluctant to share credit for team successes, and avoids collaboration to protect his own interests. This behavior leads to strained relationships, lower team morale, and missed opportunities for innovation.

2. Personal Development:

- Abundance Mentality: Lisa believes that there is always room for growth and improvement. She embraces new challenges, seeks out learning opportunities, and is open to feedback. Lisa's growth mindset leads to continuous personal and professional development, increased resilience, and a high level of effectiveness.

- Scarcity Mentality: Mark fears that he isn't good enough and worries that others are more capable. He avoids taking risks, resists change, and is defensive when receiving feedback. This scarcity mindset limits Mark's growth, reduces his effectiveness, and leads to a stagnant career.

The difference between an abundance mentality and a scarcity mentality is profound, influencing how we perceive the world, interact with others, and approach challenges. An abundance mentality fosters creativity, collaboration, resilience, and fulfillment, leading to greater effectiveness in all areas of life. In contrast, a scarcity mentality breeds fear, competition, and dissatisfaction, limiting one's potential and effectiveness.

By cultivating an abundance mentality—through practices such as gratitude, embracing a growth mindset, focusing on possibilities, cultivating generosity, and building trust—you can enhance your effectiveness, build stronger relationships, and lead a more fulfilling life.

As you adopt this mindset, you will find that opportunities are abundant, challenges are surmountable, and success is a shared experience. The shift from scarcity to abundance is a powerful transformation that can unlock your full potential and pave the way for lasting success and happiness.

Techniques for Adopting an Abundance Mindset

Adopting an abundance mindset can transform the way you approach life, relationships, and challenges. This mindset is characterized by the belief that there is more than enough success, opportunities, and resources to go around, and it fosters a positive, proactive approach to life. Shifting from a scarcity mindset, which is driven by fear and competition, to an abundance mindset requires intentional effort and consistent practice. In this chapter, we will explore practical techniques that can help you cultivate an abundance mindset, leading to greater fulfillment, resilience, and effectiveness in all areas of your life.

1. Practice Gratitude Daily

Gratitude is the foundation of an abundance mindset. When you focus on what you have, rather than what you lack, you cultivate a sense of contentment and positivity that reinforces the belief that life is abundant.

Techniques for Practicing Gratitude:

- Keep a Gratitude Journal: Set aside a few minutes each day to write down three to five things you are grateful for. These can be as simple as a sunny day, a supportive friend, or a successful project at work. Reflecting on the positive aspects of your life helps shift your focus from scarcity to abundance.

- Express Gratitude to Others: Take the time to express your gratitude to the people in your life. Whether it's a handwritten note, a text message, or a verbal acknowledgment, letting others know that you appreciate them fosters positive relationships and reinforces an abundance mindset.

- Focus on the Present Moment: Gratitude is often found in the present moment. Practice mindfulness by taking a few deep breaths and observing your surroundings. Notice the beauty, comfort, or joy in the small details of your life, and allow yourself to feel grateful for them.

2. Reframe Challenges as Opportunities

An abundance mindset views challenges not as threats, but as opportunities for growth and learning. By reframing difficulties in this way, you can approach them with optimism and resilience.

Techniques for Reframing Challenges:

- Ask Empowering Questions: When faced with a challenge, ask yourself empowering questions such as, "What can I learn from this situation?" or "How can I grow as a result of this experience?" These questions shift your focus from the problem to potential solutions and growth opportunities.

- Embrace a Growth Mindset: Adopting a growth mindset means believing that your abilities and intelligence can be developed through effort and learning. View challenges as stepping stones to improvement, and remind yourself that setbacks are temporary and can lead to personal and professional growth.

- Visualize Success: Use visualization techniques to imagine yourself successfully overcoming the challenge. Picture the steps you will take, the resources you will use, and the positive outcomes that will result. Visualization helps build confidence and reinforces the belief that you can turn challenges into opportunities.

3. Cultivate Generosity

Generosity is a key component of an abundance mindset. When you give freely—whether it's your time, knowledge, or resources—you reinforce the belief that there is more than enough to go around.

Techniques for Cultivating Generosity:

- Share Your Knowledge and Skills: Look for opportunities to mentor, teach, or share your expertise with others. Whether it's helping a colleague with a project, offering advice to a friend, or volunteering in your community, sharing what you know strengthens your connections and reinforces an abundance mentality.

- Practice Acts of Kindness: Small acts of kindness, such as buying coffee for a coworker, helping a neighbor with groceries, or sending a thoughtful message to a friend, create a ripple effect of positivity. These acts remind you that you have the power to make a difference, no matter how small, and that there is enough goodness in the world to be shared.

- Donate to Causes You Care About: Consider giving to charities, organizations, or causes that align with your values. Whether it's a financial contribution, donating your time, or offering resources, giving back reinforces the belief that abundance is meant to be shared.

4. Surround Yourself with Positive Influences

The people and environments you surround yourself with have a significant impact on your mindset. Positive influences can help you maintain an abundance mindset by encouraging growth, optimism, and collaboration.

Techniques for Surrounding Yourself with Positivity:

- Build a Supportive Network: Cultivate relationships with people who uplift and inspire you. Seek out mentors, friends, and colleagues who embody an abundance mindset and who encourage you to pursue your goals and dreams.

- Limit Exposure to Negativity: Be mindful of the media, social networks, and environments that you engage with. Limit your exposure to negative news, toxic social media interactions, or environments that breed competition and fear. Instead, focus on positive, growth-oriented content and communities.

- Join Groups that Promote Growth: Consider joining professional or personal development groups, clubs, or communities that focus on growth, collaboration, and abundance. These groups can provide valuable support, resources, and encouragement as you work to cultivate an abundance mindset.

5. Focus on Possibilities, Not Limitations

An abundance mindset is fueled by the belief in possibilities. Instead of focusing on what you can't do or what's lacking, direct your energy toward what is possible and what you can achieve.

Techniques for Focusing on Possibilities:

- Adopt Solution-Oriented Thinking: When faced with a problem, shift your focus from the problem itself to possible solutions. Ask yourself, "What are my options?" or "How can I approach this differently?" This mindset opens up new avenues for creativity and innovation.

- Set Ambitious Goals: Don't be afraid to set ambitious, stretch goals that challenge you to think big and step out of your comfort zone. These goals should inspire you to explore new possibilities and reach for higher levels of achievement.

- Embrace Curiosity and Experimentation: Cultivate a curious mindset by exploring new ideas, trying new things, and experimenting with different approaches. Curiosity drives innovation and helps you see possibilities where others see limitations.

6. Practice Self-Compassion and Forgiveness

Self-compassion and forgiveness are essential for maintaining an abundance mindset. When you treat yourself with kindness and forgive yourself for mistakes, you create space for growth, learning, and renewal.

Techniques for Practicing Self-Compassion and Forgiveness:

- Acknowledge Your Efforts: Recognize and appreciate the effort you put into your goals and daily life, even when things don't go as planned. Remind yourself that growth is a process and that setbacks are a natural part of the journey.

- Forgive Yourself for Mistakes: Instead of dwelling on past mistakes, practice forgiving yourself. Reflect on what you've learned from the experience and how you can apply that knowledge moving forward. Self-forgiveness allows you to move on with a sense of renewal and optimism.

- Speak Kindly to Yourself: Pay attention to your inner dialogue and replace self-criticism with self-encouragement. Use affirmations, such as "I am capable," "I am growing," or "I am worthy," to reinforce a positive self-image and an abundance mindset.

7. Embrace Lifelong Learning and Personal Growth

An abundance mindset is closely linked to a commitment to lifelong learning and personal growth. By continuously seeking new knowledge and skills, you reinforce the belief that there is always room to grow and improve.

Techniques for Embracing Lifelong Learning:

- Pursue Continuous Education: Take advantage of opportunities for formal and informal education, such as online courses, workshops, seminars, and reading. Expanding your knowledge and skills keeps your mind sharp and opens up new possibilities for growth and success.

- Set Personal Development Goals: Regularly set and review personal development goals that challenge you to grow in various areas of your life, such as career, health, relationships, and creativity. Setting goals gives you direction and purpose, reinforcing your commitment to growth.

- Reflect on Your Progress: Take time to reflect on your personal growth journey. Celebrate your achievements, recognize areas for improvement, and set new goals that inspire you to continue evolving. Reflection helps you stay aligned with your values and reinforces an abundance mindset.

8. Engage in Mindfulness and Meditation

Mindfulness and meditation are powerful practices for cultivating an abundance mindset. They help you stay present, reduce stress, and focus on the positive aspects of life.

Techniques for Practicing Mindfulness and Meditation:

- Start a Daily Meditation Practice: Set aside a few minutes each day to meditate. Focus on your breath, observe your thoughts without judgment, and cultivate a sense of peace and contentment. Meditation helps clear mental clutter and promotes a positive, abundance-focused mindset.

- Practice Mindful Awareness: Throughout the day, practice being fully present in each moment. Whether you're eating, working, or spending time with loved ones, bring your full attention to the experience. Mindful awareness helps you appreciate the richness of life and reinforces an abundance mentality.

- Use Affirmations During Meditation: Incorporate positive affirmations into your meditation practice. Repeating affirmations such as "I am abundant," "Opportunities are everywhere," or "I attract positivity and success" helps reprogram your subconscious mind and align your thoughts with an abundance mindset.

Real-Life Examples of Adopting an Abundance Mindset

To illustrate how these techniques can be applied, consider the following examples:

1. Career Advancement:

- Example: Jessica, a project manager, decided to shift from a scarcity mindset to an abundance mindset after realizing that her fear of competition was holding her back. She began practicing gratitude, setting ambitious goals, and embracing continuous learning. Jessica also started mentoring junior colleagues, sharing her knowledge generously. Over time, she noticed that her career began to flourish, with more opportunities for advancement and collaboration coming her way.

2. Personal Relationships:

- Example: David, a software engineer, struggled with feelings of inadequacy in his relationships. By adopting an abundance mindset, he started focusing on the positives in his relationships, practicing self-compassion, and expressing gratitude to his loved ones. David also surrounded himself with supportive friends who encouraged his personal growth. As a result, his relationships deepened, and he felt more connected and fulfilled.

Adopting an abundance mindset is a transformative process that requires intentional effort and practice. By incorporating techniques such as practicing gratitude, reframing challenges, cultivating generosity, surrounding yourself with positive influences, focusing on possibilities, practicing self-compassion, embracing lifelong learning, and engaging in mindfulness and meditation, you can shift your mindset from scarcity to abundance.

As you consistently apply these techniques, you will begin to see life through a lens of possibility, growth, and fulfillment. The abundance mindset not only enhances your effectiveness and success but also enriches your relationships, well-being, and overall quality of life. This shift in perspective opens the door to a world of opportunities, where there is always more to discover, share, and achieve.

Creating Opportunities: Strategies for Identifying and Leveraging Opportunities for Growth and Success

Opportunities for growth and success are all around us, but they often go unnoticed or untapped. Developing the ability to identify and leverage these opportunities is essential for personal and professional advancement. An abundance mentality plays a critical role in this process, as it helps you see possibilities where others see limitations and motivates you to take proactive steps toward your goals. In this chapter, we will explore strategies for creating opportunities and making the most of them to achieve growth and success.

1. Cultivate a Proactive Mindset

Being proactive means taking initiative and being prepared to act on opportunities as they arise. A proactive mindset allows you to anticipate challenges, seek out possibilities, and position yourself to take advantage of opportunities before they pass you by.

Techniques for Cultivating a Proactive Mindset:

- Set Clear Goals: Having clear, well-defined goals helps you stay focused and motivated. When you know what you want to achieve, you are more likely to recognize opportunities that align with your objectives. Regularly review and adjust your goals to ensure they remain relevant and achievable.

- Plan Ahead: Anticipate potential challenges and opportunities by planning ahead. Develop action plans for different scenarios, and stay informed about trends and changes in your industry or area of interest. Being prepared allows you to act quickly and decisively when opportunities arise.

- Take Initiative: Don't wait for opportunities to come to you—create them. This might involve volunteering for new projects at work, seeking out additional responsibilities, or proposing new ideas. By taking initiative, you demonstrate your willingness to grow and your readiness to seize opportunities.

2. Develop a Growth Mindset

A growth mindset is the belief that your abilities and intelligence can be developed through effort and learning. This mindset encourages you to embrace challenges, persist in the face of setbacks, and see failures as opportunities for growth.

Techniques for Developing a Growth Mindset:

- Embrace Challenges: View challenges as opportunities to learn and grow. Instead of avoiding difficult tasks, approach them with curiosity and a willingness to develop new skills. Recognize that growth often occurs outside your comfort zone.

- Learn from Failure: Instead of seeing failure as a dead end, view it as a valuable learning experience. Reflect on what went wrong, identify what you can do differently next time, and use this knowledge to improve. This approach turns setbacks into stepping stones toward success.

- Seek Feedback: Actively seek feedback from others to gain new perspectives and insights. Constructive feedback helps you identify areas for improvement and provides guidance on how to enhance your skills and performance.

3. Build a Strong Network

A strong professional and personal network can be a powerful source of opportunities. By connecting with others, you gain access to new ideas, resources, and support that can help you achieve your goals.

Techniques for Building a Strong Network:

- Attend Industry Events: Participate in industry conferences, seminars, workshops, and networking events. These gatherings provide opportunities to meet new people, exchange ideas, and learn about emerging trends. Building relationships at these events can lead to future collaborations, partnerships, and opportunities.

- Engage in Online Communities: Join online communities related to your field or interests, such as LinkedIn groups, forums, or social media networks. Engaging in discussions, sharing insights, and offering support to others in these communities helps you expand your network and stay informed about new opportunities.

- Nurture Relationships: Building a network isn't just about meeting new people—it's about nurturing relationships over time. Stay in touch with your contacts, offer help when you can, and express appreciation for their support. Strong, mutually beneficial relationships can lead to opportunities for collaboration, mentorship, and career advancement.

4. Stay Curious and Open-Minded

Curiosity and an open mind are essential for recognizing and creating opportunities. When you stay curious, you are more likely to explore new ideas, ask questions, and consider different perspectives, all of which can lead to the discovery of new opportunities.

Techniques for Staying Curious and Open-Minded:

- Explore New Areas of Interest: Don't limit yourself to your current field or expertise. Explore new areas of interest, whether through reading, attending workshops, or engaging in hobbies. Expanding your knowledge and experiences broadens your perspective and opens up new possibilities.

- Ask Questions: Cultivate the habit of asking questions, both of yourself and others. Questions like "What if?", "How can we improve this?", and "Is there a better way?" stimulate creative thinking and can lead to the identification of opportunities.

- Challenge Assumptions: Don't take things at face value—challenge assumptions and conventional wisdom. By questioning the status quo, you may uncover overlooked opportunities or innovative approaches to problems.

5. Leverage Technology and Innovation

Technology and innovation are powerful tools for creating and leveraging opportunities. Staying informed about technological advancements and innovative practices can help you identify new opportunities for growth and success.

Techniques for Leveraging Technology and Innovation:

- Stay Updated on Trends: Keep up with the latest technological trends and innovations in your industry. Subscribing to industry publications, attending webinars, and following thought leaders can help you stay informed about new developments that could lead to opportunities.

- Adopt New Tools: Embrace new tools and technologies that can enhance your productivity, creativity, and effectiveness. Whether it's project management software, data analytics tools, or social media platforms, leveraging technology can help you work more efficiently and open up new possibilities.

- Innovate and Experiment: Don't be afraid to experiment with new ideas and approaches. Innovation often involves taking risks and trying out new methods. By being open to innovation, you increase your chances of discovering breakthrough opportunities.

6. Take Calculated Risks

Risk-taking is often necessary to create and seize opportunities. However, successful risk-taking involves careful planning and analysis to ensure that the potential rewards outweigh the risks.

Techniques for Taking Calculated Risks:

- Assess the Risks and Rewards: Before taking a risk, carefully assess the potential risks and rewards. Consider the best-case and worst-case scenarios, and evaluate whether the potential benefits justify the risks. This analysis helps you make informed decisions.

- Start Small: If you're hesitant to take a big risk, start with smaller, more manageable risks. For example, you might test a new idea on a small scale before committing significant resources. Starting small allows you to learn from the experience and build confidence before taking larger risks.

- Learn from Experience: After taking a risk, reflect on the outcome and what you learned from the experience. Whether the risk paid off or not, there are valuable lessons to be gained that can inform your future decisions and help you take more calculated risks.

7. Focus on Continuous Improvement

Continuous improvement is the process of constantly seeking ways to enhance your skills, knowledge, and effectiveness. By committing to continuous improvement, you position yourself to recognize and create opportunities for growth.

Techniques for Focusing on Continuous Improvement:

- Set Personal Development Goals: Regularly set and review goals for your personal and professional development. These goals should challenge you to improve in specific areas, such as communication, leadership, or technical skills. Achieving these goals enhances your capabilities and increases your value in the marketplace.

- Seek Out Learning Opportunities: Take advantage of opportunities for learning and development, such as courses, workshops, mentorship, and on-the-job training.

Continuously updating your skills and knowledge keeps you competitive and opens up new opportunities.

- Embrace Feedback: Actively seek and embrace feedback from others, whether it's from colleagues, mentors, or customers. Constructive feedback provides valuable insights into areas where you can improve, helping you stay on the path of continuous growth.

8. Act on Opportunities with Confidence

Identifying opportunities is only the first step—you must also have the confidence to act on them. Confidence comes from believing in your abilities and trusting that you can navigate the challenges that come with pursuing opportunities.

Techniques for Acting on Opportunities with Confidence:

- Build Self-Confidence: Work on building your self-confidence by setting and achieving small goals, practicing positive self-talk, and reflecting on your past successes. Confidence in your abilities empowers you to take action when opportunities arise.

- Visualize Success: Use visualization techniques to imagine yourself successfully pursuing and achieving the opportunities you've identified. Visualization helps reinforce your belief in your ability to succeed and prepares you mentally for the steps you need to take.

- Take Decisive Action: Once you've identified an opportunity and assessed its potential, take decisive action. Avoid overthinking or second-guessing yourself—trust your judgment and move forward with determination. Taking action is often the most critical step in turning an opportunity into success.

Real-Life Examples of Creating and Leveraging Opportunities

To illustrate how these strategies can be applied, consider the following examples:

1. Entrepreneurship:

- Example: Maria, an aspiring entrepreneur, noticed a growing demand for eco-friendly products in her community. By staying curious, attending industry events, and networking with like-minded individuals, she identified an opportunity to start a business offering sustainable home goods. Maria took calculated risks, leveraged technology to market her products, and continuously sought feedback to improve her offerings. Her proactive approach and growth mindset helped her turn this opportunity into a successful business.

2. Career Advancement:

- Example: John, a software developer, wanted to advance in his career but felt stuck in his current role. By setting clear goals, seeking out mentorship, and continuously improving his technical skills, he positioned himself for new opportunities. When a challenging project opened up in his company, John took the initiative to volunteer, despite the risks involved. His proactive mindset, confidence, and willingness to take on new challenges led to a promotion and significant career growth.

Creating opportunities for growth and success requires a proactive approach, a growth mindset, and a willingness to take risks. By cultivating these qualities and applying the strategies outlined in this chapter—such as building a strong network, staying curious, leveraging technology, focusing on continuous improvement, and acting on opportunities with confidence—you can identify and capitalize on the possibilities that surround you.

Opportunities are not just something that happen to you—they are something you create through your actions, mindset, and choices. As you develop the ability to recognize and seize opportunities, you will find that the world is full of potential for growth, success, and fulfillment. With an abundance mentality guiding you, you can transform challenges into opportunities, turn ideas into achievements, and build a life rich with possibilities.

CHAPTER 09

EMBRACE CHANGE

Adapting to Change: Understanding the Dynamics of Change and Its Impact

Change is an inevitable part of life, both personally and professionally. Whether it's a shift in the workplace, a transition in personal relationships, or broader societal changes, our ability to adapt to change significantly impacts our success and well-being. Understanding the dynamics of change—how it occurs, how it affects us, and how we can navigate it effectively—is crucial for thriving in an ever-evolving world. This chapter explores the nature of change, its impact on individuals and organizations, and strategies for adapting to it with resilience and confidence.

The Nature of Change

Change is defined as the process of becoming different. It can be gradual or sudden, expected or unexpected, and it can affect individuals, groups, organizations, and societies. Understanding the nature of change helps us prepare for it and respond in ways that minimize disruption and maximize growth.

Types of Change

1. Personal Change:

   - Personal change refers to shifts in an individual's life, such as changes in relationships, health, career, or personal beliefs. These changes often require us to adapt our behaviors, attitudes, and routines to maintain balance and well-being.

2. Organizational Change:

   - Organizational change occurs within a company or institution and can include changes in leadership, structure, strategy, or technology. These changes impact employees, workflows, and the overall functioning of the organization. Successful adaptation to organizational change is critical for maintaining productivity and morale.

3. Societal Change:

   - Societal change refers to broader shifts in cultural, economic, political, or environmental conditions. These changes can influence entire communities or populations, shaping social norms, public policy, and collective behavior. Adapting to societal change often involves adjusting to new realities and finding ways to contribute positively to the community.

4. Technological Change:

- Technological change involves the introduction of new tools, systems, or processes that alter the way we live and work. Rapid advancements in technology can create both opportunities and challenges, requiring individuals and organizations to continually update their skills and adapt to new ways of doing things.

The Stages of Change

Understanding the stages of change can help us navigate the process more effectively. The stages of change, often referred to in the context of personal and organizational transformation, provide a framework for recognizing where we are in the change process and what we need to do to move forward.

1. Precontemplation:

- In this stage, individuals or organizations may be unaware of the need for change or may resist the idea of change altogether. Denial or avoidance is common, and there may be little or no intention to take action in the near future.

2. Contemplation:

- During contemplation, individuals or organizations recognize that change may be necessary and begin to weigh the pros and cons. This stage is characterized by reflection, analysis, and consideration of potential actions, but no commitment to change has been made yet.

3. Preparation:

- In the preparation stage, individuals or organizations decide to take action and begin planning for change. This stage involves setting goals, developing strategies, and gathering resources to support the change process.

4. Action:

- The action stage is when change is actively implemented. Individuals or organizations take concrete steps to modify behaviors, processes, or structures in alignment with the desired change. This stage requires effort, commitment, and often involves overcoming obstacles.

5. Maintenance:

- Maintenance involves sustaining the changes that have been made. Individuals or organizations work to reinforce new behaviors, practices, or systems, and prevent relapse into old patterns. This stage is crucial for ensuring that the change becomes permanent and integrated into daily life.

6. Termination or Integration:

- In this final stage, the change is fully integrated and becomes a natural part of the individual's or organization's routine. There is no longer any temptation to revert to old behaviors or systems, and the change is considered complete.

The Impact of Change

Change, whether positive or negative, has a profound impact on individuals and organizations. Understanding this impact helps us prepare for and manage the emotional, psychological, and practical challenges that come with change.

Impact on Individuals

1. Emotional Response:

- Change often triggers a range of emotions, including fear, anxiety, excitement, and uncertainty. These emotions can be intense, especially when the change is unexpected or involves significant life transitions. It's important to acknowledge and process these emotions to adapt effectively.

2. Stress and Resilience:

- Change can be a source of stress, particularly when it disrupts routines, relationships, or a sense of stability. However, it also provides an opportunity to build resilience—the ability to bounce back from adversity and adapt to new circumstances. Resilience is a key factor in navigating change successfully.

3. Identity and Self-Concept:

- Major changes, such as a career shift or personal loss, can impact an individual's sense of identity and self-concept. Adapting to change may involve redefining who you are, what you value, and how you see your place in the world. This process can be challenging but also deeply transformative.

4. Learning and Growth:

- Change is a powerful catalyst for learning and personal growth. It challenges us to develop new skills, adopt new perspectives, and push beyond our comfort zones. Embracing change as an opportunity for growth can lead to significant personal development and fulfillment.

Impact on Organizations

1. Productivity and Performance:

- Organizational change can disrupt workflows, alter job roles, and create uncertainty among employees. This can lead to a temporary decline in productivity and performance as individuals and teams adjust to new ways of working. Effective change management is crucial for minimizing disruption and maintaining organizational effectiveness.

2. Employee Morale and Engagement:

- How change is communicated and managed within an organization has a significant impact on employee morale and engagement. Poorly managed change can lead to confusion, fear, and disengagement, while transparent and supportive change processes can enhance trust, commitment, and motivation.

3. Innovation and Adaptability:

- Organizations that embrace change are more likely to foster a culture of innovation and adaptability. By encouraging continuous learning, open communication, and a willingness to take risks, organizations can turn change into a competitive advantage and drive long-term success.

4. Organizational Culture:

- Change often requires shifts in organizational culture—values, norms, and behaviors that define how work is done. Successfully embedding change into the organizational culture ensures that new practices are sustained and that the organization remains agile and responsive to future challenges.

Strategies for Adapting to Change

Adapting to change requires a combination of mindset, skills, and actions that enable individuals and organizations to navigate transitions effectively. The following strategies can help you embrace change with confidence and resilience.

1. Develop a Growth Mindset

A growth mindset—the belief that abilities and intelligence can be developed through effort and learning—is essential for adapting to change. By viewing change as an opportunity for growth, rather than a threat, you can approach it with curiosity, openness, and a willingness to learn.

- Embrace Challenges: See challenges as opportunities to grow and develop new skills. Instead of avoiding difficult situations, approach them with a positive attitude and a focus on learning.

- Learn from Feedback: Use feedback as a tool for growth. Whether it's positive or constructive, feedback provides valuable insights into how you can improve and adapt to change more effectively.

- Celebrate Progress: Acknowledge and celebrate your progress, no matter how small. Recognizing your achievements reinforces your growth mindset and motivates you to keep moving forward.

2. Build Resilience

Resilience is the ability to cope with and recover from adversity. Building resilience helps you navigate change with greater ease and maintain your well-being in the face of challenges.

- Practice Self-Care: Take care of your physical, emotional, and mental well-being by prioritizing sleep, exercise, healthy eating, and relaxation. Self-care strengthens your resilience and helps you manage stress more effectively.

- Stay Connected: Maintain strong relationships with friends, family, and colleagues. Social support is a key factor in resilience, providing encouragement, perspective, and assistance during times of change.

- Cultivate Flexibility: Be willing to adapt your plans and expectations as circumstances change. Flexibility allows you to navigate uncertainty with greater ease and to adjust your approach as needed.

3. Enhance Communication Skills

Effective communication is critical for navigating change, both personally and professionally. Clear, transparent communication helps reduce uncertainty, build trust, and foster collaboration.

- Listen Actively: Practice active listening by giving your full attention to others, asking clarifying questions, and reflecting on what you hear. Active listening helps you understand different perspectives and respond thoughtfully to change.

- Communicate Clearly: When communicating about change, be clear, concise, and honest. Provide as much information as possible, and address any concerns or questions directly. Clear communication reduces confusion and helps build trust.

- Encourage Dialogue: Create opportunities for open dialogue and feedback. Encourage others to share their thoughts, concerns, and ideas about the change. This collaborative approach fosters a sense of ownership and involvement in the change process.

4. Focus on Continuous Learning

Change often requires new skills, knowledge, and behaviors. Focusing on continuous learning helps you stay adaptable and prepared for whatever comes your way.

- Seek Out Learning Opportunities: Look for opportunities to learn new skills, whether through formal education, on-the-job training, or self-directed study. Continuous learning keeps you agile and ready to adapt to change.

- Embrace Lifelong Learning: Cultivate a mindset of lifelong learning by staying curious, asking questions, and seeking out new experiences. Lifelong learning keeps your mind sharp and open to new possibilities.

- Reflect on Your Experiences: Take time to reflect on your experiences with change. What have you learned? How have you grown? Reflection helps you integrate your learning and apply it to future changes.

5. Plan and Prepare

While change often brings uncertainty, planning and preparation can help you navigate transitions more smoothly.

By anticipating potential challenges and developing strategies to address them, you can reduce stress and increase your chances of success.

- Set Clear Goals: Define clear, achievable goals for how you want to navigate the change. Setting goals gives you direction and helps you stay focused on what matters most.

- Develop Action Plans: Create action plans that outline the steps you need to take to achieve your goals. Action plans provide a roadmap for navigating change and help you stay organized and on track.

- Anticipate Challenges: Consider potential challenges or obstacles that may arise during the change process. Develop contingency plans to address these challenges and minimize their impact.

6. Embrace a Positive Attitude

Your attitude toward change significantly impacts how you experience it. Embracing a positive attitude helps you approach change with confidence, optimism, and a sense of possibility.

- Focus on the Positives: Identify the potential benefits of the change, such as opportunities for growth, learning, or improvement. Focusing on the positives helps you stay motivated and resilient.

- Practice Gratitude: Cultivate gratitude by regularly reflecting on what you're thankful for, even in the midst of change. Gratitude helps shift your focus from what's difficult to what's possible.

- Stay Optimistic: Maintain a hopeful, optimistic outlook on the future. Believe that you have the resources and abilities to navigate change successfully and that good things are on the horizon.

Real-Life Examples of Adapting to Change

To illustrate how these strategies can be applied, consider the following examples:

1. Career Transition:

- Example: Emily, a marketing professional, faced a major change when her company underwent a restructuring that led to the elimination of her department. Rather than seeing this change as a setback, Emily embraced it as an opportunity to explore new career paths. She focused on continuous learning by taking courses in digital marketing, built resilience through self-care and social support, and maintained a positive attitude by setting new career goals. Within a few months, Emily secured a new position in a growing field that aligned with her passions and skills.

2. Organizational Change:

- Example: A large corporation implemented a new technology platform that required significant changes in how employees performed their jobs. The company recognized the potential for disruption and took proactive steps to help employees adapt. They provided clear communication about the change, offered extensive training and support, and encouraged open dialogue to address concerns. By focusing on continuous learning and fostering a positive attitude, the organization successfully navigated the transition, improving efficiency and employee satisfaction.

Adapting to change is an essential skill for thriving in an ever-evolving world. By understanding the dynamics of change—how it occurs, how it affects us, and how we can navigate it effectively—you can approach change with confidence and resilience.

The strategies outlined in this chapter—developing a growth mindset, building resilience, enhancing communication skills, focusing on continuous learning, planning and preparing, and embracing a positive attitude—provide a roadmap for adapting to change successfully. As you apply these strategies, you will find that change becomes less daunting and more manageable, opening up new opportunities for growth, learning, and success.

Change is not something to be feared or resisted; it is an integral part of life that brings with it the potential for transformation and renewal. By embracing change with an open heart and a proactive approach, you can navigate life's transitions with grace and confidence, emerging stronger and more capable on the other side.

Techniques for Developing Resilience and Adaptability

Resilience and adaptability are two of the most important qualities you can develop to navigate the complexities of life. Resilience refers to the ability to recover from setbacks, while adaptability is the capacity to adjust to new conditions or environments. Together, these traits enable you to face challenges head-on, bounce back from adversity, and thrive in an ever-changing world. In this chapter, we will explore practical techniques for building resilience and enhancing adaptability, providing you with the tools to face life's challenges with confidence and grace.

1. Cultivate a Growth Mindset

A growth mindset is the belief that your abilities and intelligence can be developed through effort, learning, and perseverance. This mindset is foundational for both resilience and adaptability, as it encourages you to view challenges as opportunities for growth rather than as insurmountable obstacles.

Techniques for Cultivating a Growth Mindset:

- Embrace Challenges: Instead of avoiding difficult situations, approach them as opportunities to learn and grow. When you encounter obstacles, remind yourself that these experiences can help you develop new skills and become more resilient.

- Reframe Failures: View failures not as evidence of your limitations, but as valuable learning experiences. Reflect on what went wrong, what you can learn from the situation, and how you can apply those lessons in the future. This approach fosters adaptability by encouraging continuous learning and improvement.

- Celebrate Effort and Progress: Focus on the effort you put into overcoming challenges rather than just the outcomes. Celebrate small wins and progress, which reinforces the idea that growth and development come through persistence and hard work.

2. Build Emotional Intelligence

Emotional intelligence (EI) is the ability to recognize, understand, and manage your own emotions, as well as the emotions of others. High emotional intelligence enhances resilience by helping you navigate emotional responses to stress and change, and it supports adaptability by improving your ability to connect with others and respond effectively to new situations.

Techniques for Building Emotional Intelligence:

- Practice Self-Awareness: Regularly reflect on your emotions, thoughts, and behaviors. Identify patterns in how you respond to stress and change, and consider how these patterns affect your resilience and adaptability. Increased self-awareness allows you to manage your emotions more effectively.

- Develop Empathy: Cultivate empathy by actively listening to others, trying to understand their perspectives, and recognizing their emotional needs. Empathy enhances your ability to adapt to social and environmental changes by fostering better communication and relationships.

- Improve Emotional Regulation: Learn techniques for managing your emotions, such as deep breathing, mindfulness, and cognitive reframing. By regulating your emotional responses, you can remain calm and focused during stressful situations, increasing your resilience.

3. Strengthen Your Support Network

A strong support network is a critical resource for building resilience and adaptability. Having a network of supportive relationships provides emotional support, practical assistance, and a sense of belonging, all of which are essential for navigating change and adversity.

Techniques for Strengthening Your Support Network:

- Nurture Existing Relationships: Invest time and energy in maintaining strong, positive relationships with family, friends, and colleagues. Regular communication, mutual support, and shared experiences help build trust and deepen connections.

- Expand Your Network: Seek out new relationships and connections, both personally and professionally. Join social or professional groups, attend networking events, or participate in community activities. Expanding your network increases your access to diverse perspectives, resources, and opportunities.

- Be a Source of Support: Offer support to others in your network, whether through listening, offering advice, or providing practical help. By being there for others, you reinforce reciprocal relationships and build a stronger, more resilient network.

4. Develop Problem-Solving Skills

Effective problem-solving is a key component of both resilience and adaptability. The ability to identify, analyze, and address challenges in a constructive manner allows you to navigate obstacles and adapt to new circumstances more effectively.

Techniques for Developing Problem-Solving Skills:

- Practice Critical Thinking: Enhance your problem-solving abilities by practicing critical thinking. Analyze situations from multiple perspectives, identify underlying causes, and consider potential solutions. Critical thinking helps you approach problems methodically and with an open mind.

- Break Down Problems: When faced with a complex challenge, break it down into smaller, more manageable parts. Address each part step by step, which makes the problem less overwhelming and easier to solve. This technique also helps you adapt to change by allowing you to tackle one aspect at a time.

- Stay Solution-Oriented: Focus on finding solutions rather than dwelling on the problem. Adopt a proactive mindset by asking yourself, "What can I do to address this?" or "How can I turn this challenge into an opportunity?" Staying solution-oriented encourages resilience by keeping you focused on positive action.

5. Enhance Flexibility and Adaptability

Flexibility is the ability to adjust your approach or behavior in response to changing circumstances. Enhancing your flexibility allows you to adapt more easily to new situations, roles, or environments, making you more resilient in the face of change.

Techniques for Enhancing Flexibility:

- Embrace Change: Instead of resisting change, view it as an opportunity for growth and exploration. Practice adapting to small changes in your daily routine, such as trying new activities, altering your schedule, or experimenting with different approaches to tasks.

- Cultivate Open-Mindedness: Keep an open mind when faced with new ideas, perspectives, or challenges. Being open-minded allows you to consider alternative solutions, learn from others, and adapt more easily to new situations.

- Develop Contingency Plans: Anticipate potential changes or disruptions and develop contingency plans for how you will respond. Having a backup plan in place reduces uncertainty and increases your confidence in navigating unexpected changes.

6. Practice Self-Care and Stress Management

Self-care and stress management are essential for maintaining resilience and adaptability. By taking care of your physical, mental, and emotional well-being, you build the strength and energy needed to cope with challenges and adapt to new situations.

Techniques for Practicing Self-Care and Stress Management:

- Prioritize Physical Health: Maintain a healthy lifestyle by engaging in regular exercise, eating a balanced diet, getting enough sleep, and staying hydrated. Physical health supports mental and emotional resilience, helping you stay strong in the face of adversity.

- Incorporate Relaxation Techniques: Practice relaxation techniques such as deep breathing, meditation, yoga, or progressive muscle relaxation. These techniques help reduce stress, calm the mind, and enhance your ability to manage challenging situations.

- Set Healthy Boundaries: Protect your time and energy by setting boundaries around work, relationships, and personal commitments. Healthy boundaries prevent burnout, reduce stress, and allow you to focus on activities that support your well-being.

7. Engage in Continuous Learning and Personal Development

Continuous learning and personal development are crucial for building resilience and adaptability. By continually expanding your knowledge and skills, you increase your capacity to handle new challenges, adapt to change, and seize opportunities for growth.

Techniques for Continuous Learning and Personal Development:

- Pursue New Skills and Knowledge: Regularly seek out opportunities to learn new skills or acquire new knowledge, whether through formal education, online courses, workshops, or self-directed study. Continuous learning keeps you adaptable and prepared for change.

- Reflect on Your Experiences: Take time to reflect on your past experiences, especially those involving change or adversity. Consider what you learned, how you grew, and how you can apply those lessons to future challenges. Reflection deepens your understanding and reinforces resilience.

- Set Personal Development Goals: Regularly set and review personal development goals that challenge you to grow in various areas of your life, such as career, health, relationships, and creativity. Setting goals gives you direction and purpose, reinforcing your commitment to growth.

8. Cultivate a Positive Attitude

A positive attitude is a powerful tool for building resilience and adaptability. By focusing on the positive aspects of a situation and maintaining hope for the future, you can approach challenges with greater confidence and determination.

Techniques for Cultivating a Positive Attitude:

- Practice Gratitude: Regularly reflect on what you are grateful for, even in the midst of challenges. Practicing gratitude shifts your focus from what is going wrong to what is going right, fostering a more positive outlook.

- Focus on Solutions: Instead of dwelling on problems or setbacks, direct your energy toward finding solutions and taking constructive action. Focusing on solutions keeps you motivated and helps you maintain a positive attitude.

- Surround Yourself with Positivity: Surround yourself with people, environments, and activities that uplift and inspire you. Positive influences reinforce your resilience and adaptability by providing encouragement and support.

Real-Life Examples of Resilience and Adaptability

To illustrate how these techniques can be applied, consider the following examples:

1. Career Transition:

- Example: Jessica, an accountant, faced an unexpected job loss due to company downsizing. Instead of feeling defeated, she embraced a growth mindset and viewed the situation as an opportunity to explore new career paths. Jessica pursued additional certifications in financial analysis, expanded her network through professional organizations, and sought out mentors for guidance. Her proactive approach and resilience led to a successful transition into a new role in financial consulting, where she thrived.

2. Personal Challenge:

- Example: Mark, a father of two, experienced a significant life change when he was diagnosed with a chronic illness. Rather than allowing the diagnosis to overwhelm him,

Mark focused on building resilience and adaptability. He developed a strong support network by joining a patient advocacy group, practiced stress management techniques such as meditation and exercise, and sought out information to better manage his condition. Mark's positive attitude and adaptability enabled him to maintain a high quality of life and continue to be an active, engaged parent.

Resilience and adaptability are essential qualities for navigating the complexities of life. By developing these traits, you can face challenges with confidence, recover from setbacks more quickly, and thrive in an ever-changing world.

The techniques outlined in this chapter—cultivating a growth mindset, building emotional intelligence, strengthening your support network, developing problem-solving skills, enhancing flexibility, practicing self-care, engaging in continuous learning, and cultivating a positive attitude—provide a comprehensive approach to building resilience and adaptability. As you apply these techniques, you will find that you are better equipped to handle whatever life throws your way, emerging stronger and more capable with each challenge you overcome.

Resilience and adaptability are not just about surviving change—they are about thriving in it. By embracing these qualities, you can turn challenges into opportunities, setbacks into stepping stones, and change into a catalyst for growth and success.

Leading Change: Strategies for Effectively Managing and Leading Change Initiatives

In today's dynamic world, the ability to effectively lead and manage change is crucial for any organization's success. Whether it's a shift in strategy, the implementation of new technology, or a reorganization of teams, change initiatives require strong leadership to ensure smooth transitions and positive outcomes. This chapter explores strategies for effectively managing and leading change initiatives, providing leaders with the tools to guide their teams through change with confidence and success.

1. Develop a Clear Vision and Communicate It Effectively

A successful change initiative begins with a clear and compelling vision. The vision defines the purpose of the change, what the organization aims to achieve, and how it aligns with the overall goals of the company. Effective communication of this vision is essential to get buy-in from all stakeholders and to guide the organization through the change process.

Strategies for Developing and Communicating a Clear Vision:

- Clarify the Purpose: Start by clearly defining why the change is necessary. Explain how the change will benefit the organization, its employees, and its customers. A well-defined purpose provides direction and motivation for everyone involved.

- Articulate the End Goal: Describe the desired outcome of the change initiative. What will success look like? How will the organization be different or better as a result of the change? A clear end goal helps employees understand what they are working toward and why it matters.

- Simplify the Message: Communicate the vision in simple, straightforward language that everyone can understand. Avoid jargon or overly complex explanations. The goal is to make the vision accessible and relatable to all employees.

- Use Multiple Channels: Communicate the vision through various channels—meetings, emails, presentations, and informal conversations. Repetition helps reinforce the message and ensures that everyone receives and understands the vision.

- Inspire and Motivate: A compelling vision should inspire and motivate employees. Highlight the opportunities that the change presents, such as personal growth, career advancement, or improved job satisfaction. Inspire employees by connecting the vision to their values and aspirations.

2. Build a Strong Change Leadership Team

Leading change requires a team of committed leaders who can guide the organization through the transition. A strong change leadership team is responsible for planning, implementing, and sustaining the change initiative. This team should be diverse, including individuals with different skills, perspectives, and areas of expertise.

Strategies for Building a Strong Change Leadership Team:

- Select the Right People: Choose individuals who are not only skilled and experienced but also committed to the change initiative. Look for leaders who are resilient, adaptable, and capable of influencing others. These qualities are essential for navigating the challenges of change.

- Ensure Diversity: Include team members from different departments, levels, and backgrounds. A diverse team brings a variety of perspectives and ideas, which can lead to more innovative solutions and better decision-making.

- Define Roles and Responsibilities: Clearly define the roles and responsibilities of each team member. Ensure that everyone understands their specific duties, as well as how their work contributes to the overall success of the change initiative.

- Foster Collaboration: Encourage collaboration within the change leadership team. Regular meetings, open communication, and shared goals help build trust and ensure that everyone is working together toward the same objectives.

- Empower the Team: Give the change leadership team the authority and resources they need to execute the change initiative effectively. Empowering the team fosters accountability and ensures that decisions can be made quickly and effectively.

3. Engage and Involve Stakeholders

Stakeholder engagement is critical to the success of any change initiative. Stakeholders include employees, managers, customers, and any other individuals or groups affected by the change. Engaging stakeholders early and throughout the process helps build trust, reduce resistance, and ensure that the change is implemented smoothly.

Strategies for Engaging and Involving Stakeholders:

- Identify Key Stakeholders: Identify all the stakeholders who will be affected by the change. Consider their level of influence, their concerns, and their needs. Understanding your stakeholders helps you tailor your communication and engagement strategies.

- Involve Stakeholders Early: Involve stakeholders in the change process from the beginning. Solicit their input, listen to their concerns, and address their questions. Early involvement helps build a sense of ownership and reduces resistance to the change.

- Communicate Transparently: Be transparent in your communication with stakeholders. Share information about the change, including the reasons behind it, the expected outcomes, and any potential challenges. Transparency builds trust and keeps stakeholders informed and engaged.

- Provide Opportunities for Feedback: Create opportunities for stakeholders to provide feedback throughout the change process. This could include surveys, focus groups, or one-on-one meetings. Feedback helps you identify potential issues and make adjustments as needed.

- Acknowledge and Address Concerns: Acknowledge any concerns or fears that stakeholders may have about the change. Address these concerns with empathy and provide clear, honest answers. Taking stakeholder concerns seriously helps reduce anxiety and resistance.

4. Plan and Execute the Change

A well-thought-out plan is essential for the successful execution of a change initiative. This plan should outline the steps needed to achieve the desired outcomes, identify potential risks, and include strategies for mitigating those risks. Effective execution involves careful monitoring and adjustments as needed to ensure that the change stays on track.

Strategies for Planning and Executing the Change:

- Develop a Detailed Change Plan: Create a comprehensive plan that outlines the objectives, timeline, resources, and key milestones for the change initiative. The plan should also include a clear roadmap for how the change will be implemented across the organization.

- Conduct a Risk Assessment: Identify potential risks and challenges that could arise during the change process. Develop contingency plans to address these risks and minimize their impact on the initiative.

- Allocate Resources: Ensure that the necessary resources—time, budget, personnel, and technology—are allocated to support the change initiative. Adequate resources are critical for successful implementation.

- Monitor Progress: Regularly monitor the progress of the change initiative against the plan. Use key performance indicators (KPIs) to track success and identify any areas where the plan may need to be adjusted.

- Be Flexible and Adapt: Be prepared to adapt the plan as needed based on feedback, new information, or changing circumstances. Flexibility is key to navigating the complexities of change and ensuring that the initiative remains on track.

5. Manage Resistance to Change

Resistance to change is a natural human response, but it can be a significant barrier to the success of a change initiative. Managing resistance effectively involves understanding the root causes of resistance and addressing them through communication, support, and involvement.

Strategies for Managing Resistance to Change:

- Understand the Root Causes: Identify the underlying reasons for resistance. Common causes include fear of the unknown, loss of control, lack of understanding, or concerns about the impact of the change. Understanding these causes allows you to address them more effectively.

- Communicate the Benefits: Clearly communicate the benefits of the change to those who are resistant. Help them understand how the change will positively impact their work, their team, and the organization as a whole. Emphasizing the benefits can help shift perspectives and reduce resistance.

- Provide Support: Offer support to employees who are struggling with the change. This could include additional training, one-on-one coaching, or access to resources that help them adjust to the new situation. Providing support helps employees feel more confident and capable of adapting to the change.

- Involve Employees in the Process: Involve employees in the change process by seeking their input and allowing them to participate in decision-making. When employees feel that they have a voice and a stake in the outcome, they are more likely to support the change.

- Acknowledge and Validate Feelings: Recognize that resistance is often rooted in legitimate concerns or fears. Acknowledge these feelings and validate them by listening and responding with empathy. This approach builds trust and can help reduce resistance.

6. Provide Training and Development

Effective change management often requires new skills, knowledge, and behaviors. Providing training and development opportunities is essential for ensuring that employees have the tools they need to succeed in the new environment.

Strategies for Providing Training and Development:

- Conduct a Training Needs Assessment: Identify the skills and knowledge that employees will need to successfully navigate the change. This assessment helps you tailor training programs to address specific gaps and ensure that employees are prepared for the transition.

- Offer Targeted Training Programs: Develop and deliver targeted training programs that focus on the skills and knowledge needed for the change initiative. This could include workshops, online courses, or hands-on training sessions.

- Encourage Continuous Learning: Foster a culture of continuous learning by encouraging employees to seek out additional training and development opportunities. Providing access to resources such as online learning platforms, mentoring programs, or professional development courses supports ongoing growth.

- Evaluate Training Effectiveness: Assess the effectiveness of training programs by gathering feedback from participants and measuring improvements in performance. Use this information to refine and enhance future training efforts.

7. Sustain the Change and Reinforce New Behaviors

Once the change has been implemented, it's essential to sustain the momentum and reinforce the new behaviors or practices. Sustaining change requires ongoing communication, reinforcement, and monitoring to ensure that the change becomes embedded in the organization's culture.

Strategies for Sustaining Change and Reinforcing New Behaviors:

- Communicate Ongoing Progress: Keep employees informed about the progress of the change initiative, even after the initial implementation. Regular updates reinforce the importance of the change and help maintain momentum.

- Celebrate Successes: Recognize and celebrate the successes achieved as a result of the change. Celebrations can be small or large, but they should highlight the positive impact of the change and acknowledge the efforts of those involved.

- Reinforce New Behaviors: Encourage and reinforce the new behaviors or practices that the change initiative introduced. This could involve recognizing employees who exemplify the new behaviors, providing ongoing training, or integrating the changes into performance evaluations.

- Monitor and Adjust: Continuously monitor the impact of the change to ensure that it is delivering the desired outcomes. Be prepared to make adjustments if necessary to address any challenges or barriers that arise.

- Integrate Change into the Culture: Work to integrate the change into the organization's culture by aligning it with the organization's values, mission, and long-term goals. When the change becomes part of the culture, it is more likely to be sustained over time.

Real-Life Examples of Leading Successful Change Initiatives

To illustrate how these strategies can be applied, consider the following examples:

1. Technology Implementation:

- Example: A large retail company decided to implement a new inventory management system to improve efficiency and reduce costs. The leadership team developed a clear vision for how the new system would benefit the company, communicated this vision effectively to all employees, and provided targeted training to ensure that staff could use the system confidently. Despite initial resistance, the leadership team managed to build buy-in by involving employees in the process, addressing their concerns, and celebrating early successes. As a result, the company successfully integrated the new system, leading to significant improvements in operations.

2. Organizational Restructuring:

- Example: A global manufacturing firm faced the need to restructure its operations to remain competitive in a changing market. The CEO and senior leadership team created a clear plan for the restructuring, including detailed communication strategies and stakeholder engagement initiatives. They formed a diverse change leadership team to manage the transition and worked closely with managers to ensure that employees received the support and training they needed. The leadership team also focused on sustaining the change by aligning the new structure with the company's long-term goals and integrating it into the company culture.

The restructuring was completed successfully, resulting in increased efficiency and a stronger market position.

Leading change is one of the most challenging and rewarding aspects of leadership. By developing a clear vision, building a strong leadership team, engaging stakeholders, managing resistance, providing training, and sustaining the change, leaders can effectively guide their organizations through transitions and achieve lasting success.

The strategies outlined in this chapter—communicating a clear vision, involving stakeholders, executing a detailed plan, managing resistance, offering training, and reinforcing new behaviors—provide a comprehensive approach to leading change initiatives. As you apply these strategies, you will be better equipped to lead your organization through change with confidence, resilience, and a focus on achieving positive outcomes.

Change is inevitable, but with the right leadership, it can be a powerful force for growth, innovation, and success. By embracing the challenge of leading change, you have the opportunity to shape the future of your organization and create a lasting impact that benefits everyone involved.

CHAPTER 10

LEAVE A LEGACY

Creating a Lasting Impact: The Importance of Leaving a Positive Legacy

In the course of our lives, we strive not only to achieve personal success but also to make a lasting impact on the world around us. The concept of leaving a legacy is about more than just our accomplishments; it's about the values we live by, the contributions we make to others, and the mark we leave on the world. A positive legacy is one that inspires, uplifts, and benefits future generations, ensuring that our influence endures long after we are gone. This chapter explores the importance of leaving a positive legacy and how you can actively work toward creating a lasting impact that reflects your values and aspirations.

Understanding the Concept of Legacy

A legacy is the lasting impression and impact that an individual leaves behind. It encompasses the values, contributions, and influence that continue to shape the lives of others even after the individual is no longer present. While legacies can take many forms, a positive legacy is characterized by the ways in which a person's life and actions contribute to the well-being and advancement of others.

The Elements of a Positive Legacy

1. Values and Principles:

- The values and principles that guide your decisions and actions are central to your legacy. These might include integrity, kindness, generosity, perseverance, or a commitment to justice. A positive legacy is built on the consistent application of these values throughout your life.

2. Contributions to Others:

- Your legacy is also defined by the ways in which you contribute to the lives of others. This can include mentorship, philanthropy, volunteer work, or simply acts of kindness and support. Positive contributions help others grow, succeed, and thrive, leaving a lasting impact.

3. Achievements and Accomplishments:

- While achievements and accomplishments are part of your legacy, they are most meaningful when they are aligned with your values and contribute to the greater good.

Whether it's a successful career, a groundbreaking innovation, or a community project, the legacy lies in how these achievements benefit others.

4. Relationships and Connections:

- The relationships you build and the connections you foster are key components of your legacy. Positive, supportive relationships leave a lasting impact on those you interact with, and the love, respect, and encouragement you offer others continue to resonate long after you are gone.

5. Influence and Inspiration:

- A positive legacy often involves the influence you have on others—how you inspire them to be better, to pursue their goals, and to live according to their values. This influence can be felt through your words, actions, and example, encouraging others to carry forward the principles you embodied.

The Importance of Leaving a Positive Legacy

Leaving a positive legacy is important because it ensures that your life's work and values continue to make a difference, even after you are no longer here. It's about contributing to something larger than yourself and creating a ripple effect that benefits future generations.

Reasons to Leave a Positive Legacy

1. Continuity of Values:

- By leaving a positive legacy, you help ensure that the values and principles you hold dear continue to influence and guide others. This continuity of values contributes to a better world, where the principles of integrity, kindness, and justice are upheld.

2. Inspiration for Future Generations:

- A positive legacy serves as a source of inspiration for future generations. When others see the impact of your life and the difference you made, they are motivated to follow in your footsteps, to strive for excellence, and to make their own positive contributions.

3. Creating a Lasting Impact:

- The contributions you make through your legacy have the potential to create lasting change. Whether it's through charitable work, mentorship, or innovative ideas, the impact of your actions can continue to benefit others for years to come.

4. Personal Fulfillment:

- Knowing that you have made a lasting, positive impact on the world brings a deep sense of personal fulfillment. It gives your life meaning and purpose, knowing that your efforts have contributed to the greater good and that your influence will endure.

5. Strengthening Communities:

- A positive legacy often involves strengthening communities—whether they are local, professional, or global. By contributing to the well-being and development of these communities, you help create a stronger, more supportive environment for everyone.

Strategies for Creating a Positive Legacy

Creating a positive legacy requires intentionality and a commitment to living according to your values. It involves making conscious choices that reflect the impact you want to have and taking actions that contribute to the well-being of others.

1. Define Your Values and Vision

The first step in creating a positive legacy is to define the values and vision that will guide your life. This involves reflecting on what matters most to you and how you want to be remembered.

Strategies for Defining Your Values and Vision:

- Reflect on Your Core Values: Take time to identify the core values that are most important to you. These might include honesty, compassion, creativity, or service to others. Consider how these values influence your decisions and actions, and how you can live them out more fully.

- Create a Personal Mission Statement: A personal mission statement is a concise declaration of your purpose and the impact you want to make. It should reflect your values and outline the principles that will guide your life. This statement serves as a roadmap for creating your legacy.

- Visualize Your Desired Legacy: Imagine how you want to be remembered and the impact you want to leave behind. What contributions do you want to make? How do you want to influence others? Visualization helps you clarify your vision and set goals that align with your desired legacy.

2. Live with Integrity and Purpose

Living with integrity means consistently aligning your actions with your values, even when it's difficult. Purpose-driven living involves pursuing goals and activities that contribute to your legacy and bring meaning to your life.

Strategies for Living with Integrity and Purpose:

- Align Actions with Values: Regularly assess whether your actions align with your values. When faced with decisions, ask yourself how each option reflects your core principles. Consistency in your actions builds trust and credibility, which are essential for a positive legacy.

- Pursue Meaningful Goals: Set goals that are meaningful and aligned with your vision for your legacy. These goals should contribute to the well-being of others, advance your personal growth, and reflect your commitment to making a positive impact.

- Practice Accountability: Hold yourself accountable for living according to your values and principles. Regularly review your actions and decisions, and make adjustments when necessary to stay true to your vision. Accountability helps ensure that you remain on the path to creating a positive legacy.

3. Contribute to the Well-Being of Others

One of the most powerful ways to leave a positive legacy is by contributing to the well-being of others. This can take many forms, from acts of kindness and mentorship to philanthropy and community service.

Strategies for Contributing to the Well-Being of Others:

- Engage in Community Service: Actively participate in community service projects that align with your values. Whether it's volunteering at a local charity, organizing events, or supporting social causes, community service allows you to make a direct impact on the lives of others.

- Mentor and Support Others: Share your knowledge, skills, and experience with others by becoming a mentor. Whether you mentor young professionals, students, or peers, your guidance can have a lasting impact on their personal and professional development.

- Practice Generosity: Be generous with your time, resources, and talents. Whether it's through financial contributions, sharing your expertise, or offering emotional support, generosity strengthens relationships and creates a positive ripple effect.

4. Build Strong and Positive Relationships

The relationships you build are a key component of your legacy. Positive, supportive relationships leave a lasting impact on the people you interact with and contribute to a sense of community and belonging.

Strategies for Building Strong and Positive Relationships:

- Foster Connection and Empathy: Make an effort to connect with others on a deeper level by practicing empathy and active listening. Show genuine interest in their lives, and offer support and encouragement. Strong connections are built on trust and mutual respect.

- Invest in Relationships: Invest time and energy in maintaining and nurturing your relationships. Regular communication, acts of kindness, and shared experiences strengthen bonds and create lasting memories.

- Leave a Positive Impression: Strive to leave a positive impression on everyone you meet, whether it's through a kind word, a helpful gesture, or simply being present. Positive interactions contribute to your legacy and inspire others to do the same.

5. Create and Share Knowledge

Another powerful way to leave a legacy is by creating and sharing knowledge that can benefit others. This could involve writing, teaching, or developing new ideas and innovations that advance your field or contribute to societal progress.

Strategies for Creating and Sharing Knowledge:

- Write and Publish: Share your insights, experiences, and expertise through writing. Whether it's books, articles, or blogs, written work allows you to reach a wide audience and leave a lasting intellectual legacy.

- Teach and Educate: Share your knowledge through teaching or training others. Whether you're an educator, a trainer, or simply someone with valuable experience, teaching allows you to pass on your knowledge and skills to future generations.

- Innovate and Create: Contribute to the advancement of your field or community by developing new ideas, products, or solutions. Innovation not only leaves a lasting impact but also inspires others to think creatively and push the boundaries of what's possible.

6. Reflect and Adjust Regularly

Creating a legacy is an ongoing process that requires regular reflection and adjustment. As you grow and evolve, your values and vision may change, and it's important to revisit and refine your approach to ensure that you remain aligned with your desired legacy.

Strategies for Reflecting and Adjusting:

- Regularly Review Your Legacy Goals: Take time to reflect on your legacy goals and assess your progress. Are you living according to your values? Are you making the impact you desire? Regular reviews help you stay on track and make necessary adjustments.

- Seek Feedback from Others: Ask for feedback from trusted friends, family, or mentors about how they perceive your actions and impact. This feedback can provide valuable insights into how you are viewed by others and where you can improve.

- Adapt to Change: Be open to adapting your legacy goals as your circumstances or perspectives change. Flexibility allows you to continue making a positive impact, even as your life or the world around you evolves.

Real-Life Examples of Leaving a Positive Legacy

To illustrate how these strategies can be applied, consider the following examples:

1. Philanthropy and Community Impact:

- Example: John, a successful entrepreneur, wanted to leave a legacy that reflected his commitment to education and social justice. He established a foundation that provides scholarships to underprivileged students and funds educational programs in underserved communities. John's philanthropic efforts have created opportunities for countless individuals to achieve their goals and contribute to society, ensuring that his legacy of generosity and commitment to education endures.

2. Mentorship and Knowledge Sharing:

- Example: Maria, a seasoned professional in the technology industry, dedicated her later years to mentoring young women in STEM fields. She offered guidance, shared her experiences, and helped them navigate the challenges of their careers. Maria also authored several books on leadership and innovation, leaving a wealth of knowledge for future generations. Her legacy is one of empowerment, mentorship, and a lasting impact on the tech community.

Leaving a positive legacy is about more than just achieving success—it's about making a meaningful, lasting impact on the world around you. By defining your values, living with integrity, contributing to the well-being of others, building strong relationships, sharing knowledge, and regularly reflecting on your goals, you can create a legacy that inspires and benefits future generations.

The importance of leaving a positive legacy lies in the continuity of values, the inspiration you provide to others, and the lasting impact you create. As you focus on these elements, you will find that your life's work takes on greater meaning and purpose, and your influence will continue to shape the world long after you are gone.

Ultimately, a positive legacy is a gift to the future. It's a testament to the life you lived, the principles you stood for, and the difference you made. By embracing the responsibility of leaving a positive legacy, you contribute to a better world and ensure that your impact will be felt for generations to come.

Techniques for Making a Meaningful Contribution to Your Community and Field

Making a meaningful contribution to your community and field is an essential aspect of leaving a lasting legacy. Whether through your professional work, volunteer efforts, or personal initiatives, your contributions can create positive change, inspire others, and strengthen the communities and industries you are part of. This chapter explores practical techniques for making meaningful contributions that reflect your values, expertise, and commitment to the greater good.

1. Identify Your Strengths and Passions

One of the first steps to making a meaningful contribution is understanding where your strengths and passions lie. By aligning your contributions with what you are naturally good at and what you care deeply about, you maximize your impact and find greater fulfillment in your efforts.

Techniques for Identifying Your Strengths and Passions:

- Self-Reflection: Take time to reflect on your skills, talents, and areas of expertise. What do you excel at? What activities or subjects energize and excite you? Understanding your strengths helps you identify where you can make the most significant impact.

- Seek Feedback: Ask for feedback from colleagues, friends, and mentors about what they perceive as your strengths. Sometimes, others can see talents and abilities that you might overlook. Their insights can help you gain a clearer understanding of your unique contributions.

- Explore Your Interests: Consider the issues, causes, or fields that you are passionate about. What problems do you want to solve? What changes would you like to see in your community or industry? Aligning your contributions with your passions ensures that you are motivated and committed to making a difference.

2. Set Clear Goals and Prioritize Your Efforts

To make a meaningful contribution, it's essential to set clear goals and prioritize your efforts. By defining what you want to achieve and focusing your energy on specific initiatives, you can create a more significant and lasting impact.

Techniques for Setting Clear Goals and Prioritizing Your Efforts:

- Define Your Contribution Goals: Clearly articulate what you want to contribute to your community or field. These goals should be specific, measurable, achievable, relevant, and time-bound (SMART). For example, if you are passionate about education, your goal might be to develop a mentorship program for underserved students within the next year.

- Prioritize High-Impact Activities: Evaluate your goals and identify the activities that will have the most significant impact. Focus on initiatives that align with your strengths, passions, and the needs of your community or field. Prioritizing high-impact activities ensures that your efforts are directed toward meaningful outcomes.

- Create an Action Plan: Develop a step-by-step action plan to achieve your contribution goals. Break down your goals into manageable tasks, set deadlines, and allocate resources as needed. An action plan helps you stay organized and ensures that you make steady progress toward your objectives.

3. Engage in Collaborative Efforts

Collaboration is a powerful way to amplify your contributions. By working with others who share your goals and values, you can pool resources, share knowledge, and achieve more significant results than you could on your own.

Techniques for Engaging in Collaborative Efforts:

- Build Partnerships: Identify individuals, organizations, or groups that share your vision and goals. Reach out to them to explore potential collaborations. Building partnerships allows you to combine your strengths and resources to achieve common objectives.

- Join Community or Professional Groups: Become an active member of community organizations, professional associations, or industry groups. These platforms provide opportunities to connect with like-minded individuals, share ideas, and collaborate on projects that benefit your community or field.

- Leverage Collective Impact: Participate in collective impact initiatives, where multiple organizations or stakeholders work together to address complex social or industry challenges. By aligning your efforts with others, you contribute to a coordinated approach that can lead to systemic change.

4. Share Knowledge and Expertise

One of the most meaningful ways to contribute to your community and field is by sharing your knowledge and expertise. Whether through teaching, mentoring, writing, or speaking, sharing what you know can empower others, advance your field, and leave a lasting impact.

Techniques for Sharing Knowledge and Expertise:

- Mentor Others: Offer to mentor individuals who are new to your field or who could benefit from your experience. Mentorship provides guidance, support, and encouragement, helping others develop their skills and achieve their goals.

- Teach or Train: Consider teaching a course, conducting workshops, or leading training sessions in your area of expertise. Teaching allows you to pass on valuable knowledge and skills to others, contributing to the growth and development of your community or industry.

- Write and Publish: Share your insights and expertise through writing. Whether it's articles, blogs, books, or research papers, writing allows you to reach a broader audience and contribute to the body of knowledge in your field.

- Speak and Present: Participate in conferences, seminars, or public speaking events where you can share your knowledge and ideas. Speaking engagements provide a platform to influence others, spark discussions, and inspire action.

5. Address Community and Industry Needs

A meaningful contribution often involves addressing the specific needs of your community or industry. By identifying and responding to these needs, you can create targeted initiatives that lead to tangible improvements and positive change.

Techniques for Addressing Community and Industry Needs:

- Conduct Needs Assessments: Start by conducting a needs assessment to identify the most pressing issues or challenges facing your community or industry. This could involve surveys, interviews, focus groups, or research. Understanding the needs allows you to tailor your contributions to where they are most needed.

- Develop Targeted Solutions: Based on the needs assessment, develop targeted solutions that address the root causes of the issues identified. Whether it's launching a new program, advocating for policy changes, or providing resources, your solutions should be practical and focused on creating positive change.

- Measure and Evaluate Impact: Regularly measure and evaluate the impact of your initiatives to ensure that they are effectively addressing the needs. Collect feedback, analyze outcomes, and make adjustments as necessary. Continuous evaluation helps you refine your approach and maximize the impact of your contributions.

6. Advocate for Positive Change

Advocacy is a powerful way to contribute to your community and field by influencing public opinion, policies, and practices. By raising awareness and championing causes that align with your values, you can drive meaningful change on a broader scale.

Techniques for Advocating for Positive Change:

- Raise Awareness: Use your platform to raise awareness about important issues in your community or field. This could involve writing opinion pieces, participating in public discussions, or using social media to spread the word. Raising awareness helps educate others and mobilize support for positive change.

- Engage in Policy Advocacy: Advocate for policy changes that address systemic issues or improve conditions in your community or field. This might involve working with policymakers, joining advocacy groups, or participating in campaigns. Policy advocacy can lead to lasting change that benefits a wide range of people.

- Lead by Example: Demonstrate your commitment to positive change through your actions and behavior. By living according to your values and making ethical choices, you set an example for others to follow and inspire them to take action.

7. Invest in Long-Term Initiatives

Long-term initiatives are those that have the potential to create sustained impact over time. By investing in long-term projects or programs, you can contribute to lasting change that continues to benefit your community or field for years to come.

Techniques for Investing in Long-Term Initiatives:

- Support Sustainable Projects: Focus on projects or programs that are designed for sustainability. This could involve initiatives that promote environmental stewardship, economic development, or social equity. Sustainable projects create lasting benefits and address long-term challenges.

- Establish Endowments or Funds: Consider establishing endowments, scholarships, or charitable funds that provide ongoing support for causes you care about. These financial instruments can continue to generate resources and support initiatives long after your initial contribution.

- Create Legacy Programs: Develop programs or initiatives that are designed to be continued by future generations. Legacy programs might involve education, mentorship, or community development efforts that are passed down and sustained over time.

Real-Life Examples of Making Meaningful Contributions

To illustrate how these techniques can be applied, consider the following examples:

1. Community Development:

- Example: Sarah, an architect passionate about sustainable design, identified a need for affordable housing in her city. She partnered with local nonprofits and community organizations to design and build eco-friendly, affordable homes for low-income families. Through her efforts, Sarah not only addressed a critical community need but also set a new standard for sustainable housing, leaving a lasting impact on her community.

2. Professional Advocacy:

- Example: David, a healthcare professional, noticed that mental health services were underfunded and stigmatized in his region. He began advocating for increased funding and better access to mental health care. David wrote articles, spoke at conferences, and worked with policymakers to implement new mental health initiatives. His advocacy efforts led to significant improvements in mental health services and awareness in his community.

Making a meaningful contribution to your community and field is a powerful way to leave a lasting legacy. By identifying your strengths and passions, setting clear goals, engaging in collaborative efforts, sharing knowledge, addressing community needs, advocating for change, and investing in long-term initiatives, you can create positive, lasting impact that benefits others and strengthens the world around you.

The techniques outlined in this chapter provide a roadmap for making contributions that reflect your values and expertise. As you apply these techniques, you will find that your efforts not only improve the lives of others but also bring a deep sense of fulfillment and purpose to your own life.

Ultimately, the contributions you make today will shape the future of your community and field, creating a legacy that endures for generations to come. By committing to making meaningful contributions, you ensure that your life's work continues to inspire, uplift, and benefit others long after you are gone.

Mentoring and Inspiring Others: Strategies for Guiding and Motivating Others to Achieve Their Potential

Mentoring and inspiring others is one of the most powerful ways to leave a lasting legacy. By guiding and motivating individuals to achieve their potential, you contribute not only to their personal and professional growth but also to the betterment of society as a whole. Mentoring fosters knowledge transfer, personal development, and the cultivation of future leaders. This chapter explores strategies for effectively mentoring and inspiring others, ensuring that your influence endures through the success and achievements of those you help guide.

1. Establish Trust and Build Relationships

The foundation of effective mentoring is a strong, trusting relationship between the mentor and mentee. Trust allows for open communication, vulnerability, and a supportive environment where the mentee feels comfortable seeking guidance and sharing challenges.

Strategies for Establishing Trust and Building Relationships:

- Be Approachable and Open: Make yourself accessible and approachable to your mentee. Demonstrate that you are genuinely interested in their growth and well-being. Openness and approachability encourage your mentee to share their thoughts, concerns, and aspirations with you.

- Listen Actively: Practice active listening by giving your full attention to your mentee during conversations. Listen not only to their words but also to the emotions and underlying messages they are conveying. Active listening shows that you value their perspective and are fully engaged in their development.

- Respect Confidentiality: Maintain confidentiality in your mentoring relationship. Ensure that your mentee knows they can trust you with sensitive information. Respecting confidentiality fosters a safe space for honest discussions and personal growth.

- Be Consistent and Reliable: Follow through on your commitments and be consistent in your interactions with your mentee. Reliability builds trust and demonstrates your dedication to their success.

2. Set Clear Expectations and Goals

Effective mentoring involves setting clear expectations and goals for the mentoring relationship. Establishing these parameters helps both the mentor and mentee stay focused, measure progress, and achieve desired outcomes.

Strategies for Setting Clear Expectations and Goals:

- Define the Purpose of the Relationship: Begin by discussing the purpose and objectives of the mentoring relationship. What does the mentee hope to achieve? What areas of growth are they focusing on? Clearly defining the purpose sets the direction for your mentoring efforts.

- Set SMART Goals: Work with your mentee to set Specific, Measurable, Achievable, Relevant, and Time-bound (SMART) goals. These goals should align with the mentee's aspirations and provide a clear roadmap for their development. Regularly review and adjust these goals as needed.

- Clarify Roles and Responsibilities: Discuss and clarify the roles and responsibilities of both the mentor and mentee. What is expected from each party? How will you work together to achieve the mentee's goals? Clear expectations prevent misunderstandings and ensure a productive partnership.

- Establish a Timeline: Agree on a timeline for the mentoring relationship, including regular check-ins and progress reviews. A timeline helps keep the relationship on track and provides structure to the mentoring process.

3. Provide Guidance and Support

As a mentor, your primary role is to provide guidance and support that empowers your mentee to achieve their potential. This involves offering advice, sharing knowledge, and helping them navigate challenges and opportunities.

Strategies for Providing Guidance and Support:

- Share Your Knowledge and Experience: Draw on your own experiences and expertise to provide valuable insights and advice. Share stories of your successes and challenges, and explain how you overcame obstacles. Your experiences can offer valuable lessons and inspiration to your mentee.

- Offer Constructive Feedback: Provide constructive feedback that is specific, actionable, and focused on growth. Highlight areas where your mentee is excelling, as well as areas where they can improve. Feedback should be delivered with empathy and encouragement, helping your mentee grow without discouraging them.

- Encourage Self-Reflection: Guide your mentee to reflect on their experiences, decisions, and actions. Encourage them to consider what they have learned, how they can apply these lessons in the future, and what steps they can take to continue their growth. Self-reflection fosters self-awareness and personal development.

- Help Them Navigate Challenges: Assist your mentee in navigating challenges by offering practical advice and emotional support. Whether it's dealing with a difficult situation at work, making a major decision, or overcoming personal obstacles, your guidance can help them find solutions and build resilience.

4. Foster Independence and Empowerment

A key goal of mentoring is to empower your mentee to take ownership of their development and make independent decisions. While your guidance is valuable, it's important to encourage them to think critically, take initiative, and develop their problem-solving skills.

Strategies for Fostering Independence and Empowerment:

- Encourage Critical Thinking: Challenge your mentee to think critically about the decisions they make and the actions they take. Ask probing questions that prompt them to consider different perspectives and potential outcomes. Critical thinking helps them develop the ability to analyze situations and make informed decisions.

- Promote Self-Reliance: Encourage your mentee to take initiative and solve problems on their own. While it's important to provide guidance, resist the urge to solve every problem for them. Instead, offer suggestions and let them explore solutions independently. This approach builds confidence and self-reliance.

- Celebrate Their Achievements: Acknowledge and celebrate your mentee's successes, both big and small. Celebrating achievements reinforces their confidence and motivates them to continue striving for excellence. It also helps them recognize their own capabilities and the progress they've made.

- Encourage Lifelong Learning: Instill a passion for lifelong learning in your mentee. Encourage them to seek out new opportunities for growth, whether through formal education, self-directed study, or experiential learning. Lifelong learning empowers them to continue developing their skills and knowledge long after the mentoring relationship ends.

5. Inspire by Example

Mentoring is not just about what you say but also about how you live your own life. Leading by example is one of the most powerful ways to inspire others. When your actions align with your values and principles, you demonstrate the qualities you want to instill in your mentee.

Strategies for Inspiring by Example:

- Model Integrity and Ethical Behavior: Live with integrity and uphold ethical standards in all aspects of your life. Demonstrating honesty, fairness, and accountability in your actions shows your mentee the importance of these values and inspires them to do the same.

- Show Resilience in Adversity: Share how you handle challenges and setbacks with resilience and determination. Your ability to persevere in the face of adversity serves as a powerful example for your mentee, showing them that setbacks are opportunities for growth.

- Practice Continuous Improvement: Demonstrate a commitment to personal and professional growth by continuously seeking to improve yourself. Whether it's learning new skills, seeking feedback, or striving for excellence, your dedication to growth sets a positive example for your mentee.

- Exhibit Compassion and Empathy: Show compassion and empathy in your interactions with others. Treating people with kindness and understanding creates a positive environment and encourages your mentee to cultivate these qualities in their own relationships.

6. Adapt Your Mentoring Style

Every mentee is unique, and effective mentoring requires flexibility and adaptability. Tailor your mentoring approach to meet the individual needs, preferences, and learning styles of your mentee. This personalized approach ensures that the mentoring relationship is both meaningful and effective.

Strategies for Adapting Your Mentoring Style:

- Assess Learning Styles: Take time to understand your mentee's preferred learning style. Do they learn best through hands-on experience, visual aids, or verbal discussions? Adapt your mentoring approach to align with their learning style, making it easier for them to absorb and apply new information.

- Be Flexible in Your Approach: Be willing to adjust your mentoring style as needed to accommodate changes in your mentee's goals, circumstances, or challenges. Flexibility allows you to provide the most relevant and effective support throughout the mentoring relationship.

- Encourage Open Communication: Create an environment where your mentee feels comfortable providing feedback about the mentoring process. Encourage them to share their thoughts on what's working well and what could be improved. Open communication helps you adapt your approach to better meet their needs.

- Provide Varied Experiences: Expose your mentee to a variety of experiences, perspectives, and challenges. This could involve introducing them to different aspects of your field, involving them in new projects, or connecting them with other professionals. Varied experiences broaden their horizons and help them develop a well-rounded skill set.

7. Leave Room for Growth Beyond the Mentorship

A successful mentoring relationship equips the mentee with the tools and mindset needed to continue growing and succeeding even after the formal mentorship ends. It's important to prepare your mentee for this transition and to encourage ongoing development.

Strategies for Leaving Room for Growth Beyond the Mentorship:

- Encourage Continued Networking: Help your mentee build a strong professional network that they can rely on for support and guidance in the future. Introduce them to other professionals in your field, and encourage them to actively seek out new connections.

- Promote Self-Directed Learning: Encourage your mentee to take charge of their own learning and development. Provide them with resources, such as books, courses, or industry publications, that they can use to continue growing independently.

- Discuss Long-Term Goals: Before the mentorship ends, discuss your mentee's long-term goals and how they can continue working toward them. Offer guidance on how to set and achieve these goals, and encourage them to revisit and adjust their goals as they progress.

- Foster a Growth Mindset: Instill a growth mindset in your mentee, emphasizing the importance of embracing challenges, learning from failures, and continuously striving for improvement. A growth mindset empowers them to keep growing and adapting throughout their career

Real-Life Examples of Effective Mentoring

To illustrate how these strategies can be applied, consider the following examples:

1. Career Mentorship:

- Example: Emily, a marketing executive, took on a mentorship role with a junior colleague, Rachel. Emily focused on building a trusting relationship with Rachel, offering guidance on developing her skills and navigating workplace challenges. She encouraged Rachel to set clear career goals and provided feedback on her progress. Over time, Rachel became more confident in her abilities, took on leadership roles, and eventually advanced to a management position. Emily's mentorship played a crucial role in Rachel's professional growth.

2. Personal Development Mentorship:

- Example: John, a seasoned entrepreneur, mentored a young startup founder, Alex. John shared his experiences of building businesses, provided advice on overcoming obstacles, and connected Alex with valuable contacts in the industry. He also emphasized the importance of resilience, adaptability, and ethical decision-making. Alex was inspired by John's example and applied these lessons to grow his startup into a successful company. John's mentorship not only helped Alex achieve his potential but also left a lasting impact on his approach to business and leadership.

Mentoring and inspiring others is one of the most meaningful and impactful ways to leave a legacy. By guiding and motivating individuals to achieve their potential, you contribute to their personal and professional growth and help shape the future of your community and field.

The strategies outlined in this chapter—establishing trust, setting clear goals, providing guidance, fostering independence, inspiring by example, adapting your mentoring style, and leaving room for growth—provide a comprehensive approach to effective mentoring. As you apply these strategies, you will find that your efforts not only benefit your mentees but also bring a deep sense of fulfillment and purpose to your own life.

Ultimately, the success and achievements of those you mentor are a testament to the positive impact you've made. By dedicating yourself to mentoring and inspiring others, you ensure that your legacy lives on through the individuals and leaders you help to develop, creating a ripple effect that benefits future generations.

CONCLUSION

RECAP OF THE 10 HABITS AND THEIR SIGNIFICANCE

Throughout this book, we have explored ten essential habits that contribute to personal and professional effectiveness. These habits serve as foundational principles for living a fulfilling, successful life and leaving a lasting legacy. Let's briefly recap each habit and its significance:

1. Be Proactive: Proactivity is the cornerstone of personal responsibility and control. It empowers you to take charge of your actions and decisions, shaping your destiny rather than being a victim of circumstances.

2. Begin with the End in Mind: By clarifying your vision and defining your goals, you set a clear direction for your life and work. This habit ensures that your actions align with your long-term objectives, leading to meaningful and purposeful achievements.

3. Put First Things First: Prioritizing tasks and responsibilities is key to effective time management. By focusing on what truly matters, you can achieve balance, reduce stress, and accomplish your most important goals.

4. Think Win-Win: The win-win paradigm fosters positive relationships and collaborative success. By seeking mutually beneficial solutions, you build trust and create outcomes that satisfy everyone involved.

5. Seek First to Understand, Then to Be Understood: Effective communication begins with active listening and empathy. Understanding others before expressing your own views fosters deeper connections and more productive interactions.

6. Synergize: Synergy harnesses the power of teamwork and collaboration. By integrating diverse perspectives and ideas, you can achieve results that are greater than the sum of their parts.

7. Sharpen the Saw: Continuous improvement and self-renewal are essential for long-term success. By regularly investing in your physical, mental, emotional, and spiritual well-being, you maintain the energy and resilience needed to achieve your goals.

8. Cultivate an Abundance Mentality: An abundance mentality shifts your focus from scarcity and competition to

possibilities and collaboration. This mindset encourages generosity, creativity, and a positive outlook on life.

9. Embrace Change: Adaptability and resilience are crucial in a constantly changing world. By embracing change and developing the skills to navigate it, you can turn challenges into opportunities for growth.

10. Leave a Legacy: Making a meaningful contribution to your community and field ensures that your influence endures. By mentoring others, sharing knowledge, and living according to your values, you create a lasting impact that benefits future generations.

Encouragement to Implement These Habits in Daily Life

As you reflect on these ten habits, consider how they can be integrated into your daily life. Each habit offers practical strategies for enhancing your personal and professional effectiveness, but their true power lies in consistent application. Here are a few steps you can take to begin implementing these habits:

- Start Small: Focus on one or two habits at a time. Gradually incorporate them into your routines and observe the positive changes they bring. As you become comfortable with these habits, add more to your practice.

- Set Specific Goals: Define clear, actionable goals for how you will apply each habit in your life. For example, you might set a goal to practice active listening in all your conversations or to schedule regular self-renewal activities.

- Reflect Regularly: Take time to reflect on your progress and the impact of these habits on your life. What changes have you noticed? How have these habits improved your relationships, work, or well-being? Reflection helps reinforce positive behaviors and motivates you to continue growing.

- Seek Support: Share your commitment to these habits with a friend, mentor, or colleague. Support from others can provide encouragement, accountability, and new perspectives as you work to implement these habits.

- Stay Committed: Developing new habits takes time and persistence. Stay committed to the process, even when it's challenging. Remember that the benefits of these habits—greater effectiveness, fulfillment, and a lasting legacy—are well worth the effort.

Final Thoughts on Achieving Personal and Professional Effectiveness

Achieving personal and professional effectiveness is not a destination but a continuous journey of growth and development. The habits we've explored in this book provide a roadmap for navigating this journey with purpose, integrity, and resilience.

As you implement these habits, you will likely encounter obstacles and setbacks. However, it's important to view these challenges as opportunities for learning and improvement. By staying proactive, focusing on your vision, and prioritizing what truly matters, you can overcome difficulties and continue progressing toward your goals.

Remember that personal and professional effectiveness is about more than just achieving success; it's about living a life that is meaningful, fulfilling, and aligned with your values. It's about making a positive impact on others, contributing to the greater good, and leaving a legacy that endures.

As you move forward, I encourage you to embrace these habits wholeheartedly. Let them guide your actions, inform your decisions, and shape the way you live and work. By doing so, you will not only enhance your own effectiveness but also inspire and uplift those around you.

Ultimately, the true measure of success lies not in what we accumulate but in the positive difference we make in the lives of others. By cultivating these habits, you are taking important steps toward becoming the best version of yourself and creating a legacy that will resonate for generations to come.

Resources and Tools: Recommended Reading and Tools for Further Development

To deepen your understanding of the 10 habits and further develop your personal and professional effectiveness, here is a list of recommended readings, tools, and resources. These materials offer valuable insights, practical strategies, and actionable advice to help you continue your journey toward greater effectiveness and a lasting legacy.

Recommended Reading

1. "The 7 Habits of Highly Effective People" by Stephen R. Covey

   - This foundational book is a must-read for anyone interested in personal development. Covey's principles serve as the basis for many of the habits discussed in this book, and his insights are timeless.

2. "Atomic Habits" by James Clear

- James Clear's book provides practical strategies for building good habits and breaking bad ones. His focus on small, incremental changes aligns well with the principles of proactivity and continuous improvement.

3. "Mindset: The New Psychology of Success" by Carol S. Dweck

- Carol Dweck's exploration of the growth mindset is essential reading for those looking to embrace challenges and foster resilience. Her research highlights the importance of believing in your potential for growth.

4. "Daring Greatly" by Brené Brown

- Brené Brown's work on vulnerability and courage is crucial for understanding how to build trust, connect with others, and lead effectively. Her insights are particularly relevant to the habits of empathy, communication, and leaving a legacy.

5. "Getting Things Done: The Art of Stress-Free Productivity" by David Allen

- David Allen's productivity system is highly effective for organizing tasks, managing priorities, and reducing stress. His techniques align with the principles of time management and prioritization discussed in this book.

6. "The Lean Startup" by Eric Ries

- For those interested in innovation and entrepreneurship, Eric Ries' book offers a framework for creating successful businesses by focusing on continuous improvement, adaptability, and customer feedback.

7. "Emotional Intelligence 2.0" by Travis Bradberry and Jean Greaves

   - This book provides tools and strategies for developing emotional intelligence, which is key to effective communication, leadership, and relationship-building.

8. "The Power of Habit" by Charles Duhigg

   - Charles Duhigg's exploration of the science behind habit formation provides insights into how habits work and how they can be changed. His research supports the idea that small changes in behavior can lead to significant improvements in effectiveness.

Recommended Tools and Resources

1. Personal Development Apps:

   - Habitica: A gamified habit tracker that helps you build good habits and break bad ones by turning your goals into a role-playing game.

   - Headspace: A mindfulness and meditation app that can help you practice self-care and maintain a positive, focused mindset.

   - Todoist: A task management app that helps you organize and prioritize your tasks, ensuring that you focus on what's most important.

2. Productivity Tools:

- Trello: A visual project management tool that allows you to organize tasks, set priorities, and collaborate with others.

- Evernote: A note-taking app that helps you capture ideas, organize your thoughts, and keep track of important information.

- Pomodoro Timer: A time management tool that uses the Pomodoro Technique to break work into focused intervals, helping you stay productive and manage your time effectively.

3. Learning Platforms:

- Coursera: An online learning platform offering courses on a wide range of topics, including leadership, communication, and personal development.

- LinkedIn Learning: Provides video courses taught by industry experts on skills like time management, emotional intelligence, and strategic thinking.

- Skillshare: A community-based learning platform with classes on creativity, productivity, and business skills.

4. Mentoring and Networking:

- MentorcliQ: A mentoring software platform that helps organizations implement and manage mentoring programs.

- Meetup: An online platform for finding and joining local groups that share your interests, offering opportunities for networking and collaboration.

- LinkedIn: A professional networking site that allows you to connect with others in your field, share knowledge, and find mentorship opportunities.

Case Studies and Success Stories: Real-Life Examples of Individuals and Organizations Applying the 10 Habits Effectively

To illustrate how the 10 habits can be effectively applied in real-life scenarios, here are some case studies and success stories of individuals and organizations that have embraced these principles and achieved remarkable results.

Case Study 1: A CEO's Transformation through Proactivity and Prioritization

Background:

Jane, the CEO of a mid-sized tech company, was struggling to keep up with the demands of her role. She often felt overwhelmed by the constant influx of tasks and responsibilities, and her company was experiencing stagnation in growth.

Application of Habits:

Jane decided to take a proactive approach to her situation. She began by clearly defining her vision for the company (Begin with the End in Mind) and identifying the key areas that needed her focus. She then applied the principle of Put First Things First by prioritizing her time around these critical areas, delegating tasks that were less essential, and setting boundaries to protect her focus.

Outcome:

As a result of these changes, Jane became more effective in her role. She was able to lead her company through a successful period of growth, improved her work-life balance, and gained the respect and trust of her team.

Case Study 2: A Nonprofit's Success through Collaboration and Abundance Mentality

Background:

A nonprofit organization dedicated to providing educational resources to underserved communities was struggling with limited resources and increasing demand for its services.

Application of Habits:

The organization's leadership adopted a Think Win-Win and Synergize approach by partnering with other nonprofits, local businesses, and volunteers to expand their reach and effectiveness. They also embraced an Abundance Mentality, believing that there were enough resources and opportunities to go around if they worked collaboratively.

Outcome:

Through these efforts, the nonprofit was able to significantly increase its impact, serving more communities than ever before. The partnerships they formed led to new funding opportunities, shared resources, and a stronger network of support.

Case Study 3: Personal Development through Continuous Improvement and Self-Renewal

Background:

Michael, a software engineer, felt stuck in his career and was unsure how to advance. He realized that his skills were becoming outdated and that he needed to invest in his personal growth.

Application of Habits:

Michael adopted the habit of Sharpen the Saw by dedicating time each week to learning new programming languages and attending industry conferences. He also worked on developing his soft skills, such as communication and teamwork, to become a more well-rounded professional.

Outcome:

Over time, Michael's commitment to continuous improvement paid off. He received a promotion to a leadership role, became a mentor to junior engineers, and found renewed passion and purpose in his career.

Case Study 4: A School's Transformation through Effective Communication and Leadership

Background:

A struggling public school was facing low morale among teachers, declining student performance, and a lack of engagement from parents and the community.

Application of Habits:

The school's principal decided to focus on Seek First to Understand, Then to Be Understood by holding listening sessions with teachers, students, and parents to understand their concerns and needs. She also implemented regular communication channels and encouraged a culture of open dialogue. To inspire and guide her staff, she embraced the habit of Leaving a Legacy by mentoring young teachers and fostering a sense of shared mission and purpose.

Outcome:

The school saw a significant turnaround. Teacher morale improved, student performance increased, and the school developed stronger ties with the community. The principal's leadership was credited with transforming the school into a thriving, supportive environment for both students and staff.

Final Thoughts

These case studies demonstrate the power of the 10 habits in real-world settings. Whether applied at the individual, organizational, or community level, these habits can lead to profound changes in effectiveness, satisfaction, and impact. By embracing these principles and integrating them into your daily life, you too can achieve similar success and leave a lasting legacy.

* 9 7 9 8 3 3 0 6 3 1 7 7 3 *